ROBINSON CRUSOE

By DANIEL DEFOE

With an introduction by

LORA B. PECK

Illustrated in Black and White
Color illustrations by Edward F. Cortese

HOLT, RINEHART and WINSTON, *New York*

Made in the United States of America
L. C. Card #61-8857
L – 9

Contents ℒ

INTRODUCTION	ix
THE FIRST VOYAGE	1
ADVENTURES IN AFRICA	17
LIFE AND TRAVEL IN SOUTH AMERICA	41
SALVAGE FROM THE WRECK	57
BUILDING MY HOME	72
AFTER THE EARTHQUAKE	98
MAKING A COUNTRY HOME	114
TEN YEARS OF WORK	127
FOOD AND CLOTHING	164
THE SAVAGES	174
FRIDAY	193
THE SAVAGES RETURN	223
DELIVERANCE	242

List of Color Plates

At length I spied a little cove   Inside Front Cover

I took a little voyage upon the sea   Facing Front Cover

I began to instruct him in the knowledge of the true God
     Facing Back Cover

I fitted myself for a battle, knowing that I had to do with another kind of enemy   Inside Back Cover

Introduction ✒

For all who like adventure, this book will prove an open gateway. Through it they may pass to strange adventures on the high seas and on tropic shores. With the young runaway hero they may escape from humdrum, everyday existence into a thrilling life of excitement and danger, of slavery and shipwreck. With him they may come to the desert island where, alone for twenty-four years, he manages by hard work and ingenuity to supply food, clothing, and shelter for himself. They may share his terror at the coming of the cannibals, and his joy when at last he has a companion. They may be present during the final swift-moving days, packed with peril and excitement, that end in his escape.

Let no one think that this is drawn wholly from the author's imagination. It is founded upon the experiences of Alexander Selkirk, a Scotch lad who was on a ship wrecked off the coast of Chile. The young man was tossed by the sea upon the island of Juan Fernandez, which was uninhabited at that time. He saved the supplies from the ship and lived for some years alone on the island. How much Defoe added to Selkirk's adventures cannot now be told, but there is no doubt that he interwove facts and fancies until he produced a story unparalleled for its absorbing interest.

Many books of adventure have been written since this one. Many stories have been centered around shipwreck and life on a desert island. It is interesting to note, however, that Robinson Crusoe is the beginning of all fictional adventure. Thousands of authors have followed where Defoe led, but his book still holds the place it won more than two hundred years ago. It has been translated into many languages and dialects, and it is available even in Esperanto.

One element of value in this book has often been overlooked. With the increased emphasis on the social studies in the schools has come a problem of making boys and girls understand the great significance in their daily lives of the interdependence of occupations, social groups, geographical regions, and, perhaps most important of all, of the nations of the earth. Robinson Crusoe shows in striking contrast a purely independent individual life, wresting a rudimentary and laborious existence from a somewhat kindly natural environment.

A word as to the text of this edition may not be out of place. Some long and involved sentences have been separated into two or more parts to suit modern readers. However, care has been taken to preserve the exact thought in every case. Although a few paragraphs have been eliminated, every incident in the life of Robinson Crusoe from the time he first left home until he was again settled in England is here set forth in the words and the style used by Daniel Defoe in 1719. Only such notes have been given as seemed necessary, but for the most part the unusual words and expressions can be understood from their use in the text. In the author's version there are no chapters, but in this edition it has seemed desirable to divide the text into chapters, though the division does not affect the story itself.

Here, then, is THE LIFE AND ADVENTURES OF ROBINSON CRUSOE, a book that started a new era in stories. May all the boys and girls who read it now enjoy the tale as did the old and young who read it over two hundred years ago.

—LORA B. PECK

The First Voyage ✑

I was born in the year 1632, in the city of York, of a good family, though not of that country. My father was a foreigner of Bremen, who settled first at Hull. He got a good estate by merchandise, and leaving off his trade, lived afterward at York. There he married my mother, whose relations were named Robinson, a very good family in that country. For them I was called Robinson. Our English neighbors corrupted my father's name into Crusoe, and therefore my playmates called me Robinson Crusoe.

Being the third son of the family, and not bred to any trade, my head began to be filled very early with rambling thoughts. My father, who was very ancient, had given me a competent share of learning, as far as house education and a country free school generally goes, and designed me for the law, but I would be satisfied with nothing but going to sea. My inclination to this led me so strongly against the will, nay, the commands of my father, and against all the entreaties and persuasions of my mother and other friends, that there seemed to be something fatal in that inclination leading directly to the life of misery which was to befall me.

My father, a wise and grave man, gave me serious and excellent counsel against what he foresaw was my design. He called me one morning into his chamber, where he was confined by the gout, and expostulated very warmly with me upon this subject. He asked me what reasons, more than a mere wandering inclination, I had for leaving my father's house and my native country, where I might be well introduced, and had a prospect of raising my fortune by application and industry, with a life of ease and pleasure. He told me it was for men of desperate fortunes on one hand, or of aspiring superior fortunes on the other, who went abroad upon adventures, to rise by enterprise, and make themselves famous in undertakings of a nature out of the common road. These things were all either too far above me, or too far below me; mine was the middle state. He had found by long experience that this was the best state in the world—to have neither poverty nor riches.

He bade me observe it, and I should always find that the calamities of life were shared among the upper and lower part of mankind; but that the middle station had the fewest disasters, and was not exposed to so many vicissitudes as the higher or lower part of mankind.

After this, he pressed me earnestly, and in the most affectionate manner, not to play the young man, not

to precipitate myself into miseries which
the station of life I was born in, seemed to h...
vided against. He reminded me that I was under
necessity of seeking my bread; that he would do well
for me, and endeavor to enter me fairly into the station of life which he had just been recommending
to me.

He pointed out to me that if I was not very easy
and happy in the world, it must be my mere fate or
fault that must hinder it, and that he should have
nothing to answer for, having thus discharged his duty
in warning me against measures which he knew would
be to my hurt; in a word, that as he would do very
kind things for me if I would stay and settle at home
as he directed, so he would not have so much hand in
my misfortunes as to give me any encouragement to
go away.

My father went on to say that he would not cease
to pray for me, yet he would venture to say to me
that if I did take this foolish step, God would not
bless me, and I would have leisure hereafter to reflect
upon having neglected his counsel when there might
be none to assist in my recovery.

I was sincerely affected with this discourse, as, indeed, who could be otherwise, and I resolved not to
think of going abroad any more, but to settle at home
according to my father's desire. But, alas! a few days
wore it all off, and, in short, to prevent any of my
father's further importunities, a few weeks afterward
I resolved to run quite away from him. However,

I did not act so hastily as my first heat of resolution prompted, but I took my mother, at a time when I thought her a little pleasanter than ordinary, and told her that my thoughts were so entirely bent upon seeing the world that I should never settle to anything with resolution enough to go through with it, and my father had better give me his consent than force me to go without it. I told her that I was now eighteen years old, which was too late to go apprentice to a trade, or clerk to an attorney. Moreover, I was sure that, if I did, I should never serve out my time, and I should certainly run away from my master before my time was out, and go to sea. I assured her that if she would speak to my father to let me go but one voyage abroad, if I came home again and did not like it, I would go no more, and I would promise by a double diligence to recover that time I had lost.

This put my mother into a great passion. She told me that she knew it would be to no purpose to speak to my father upon any such subject. He knew too well what was my interest to give his consent to anything so much for my hurt. She wondered how I could think of any such thing after such a discourse as I had had from my father, and such kind and tender expressions as she knew my father had used to me. She said that, in short, if I would ruin myself, there was no help for me, but I might depend I should never have their consent to it. For her part she would not have so much hand in my destruction, and I should never have it to say that my mother was willing when my father was not.

Though my mother refused to ask my father's permission, yet, as I heard afterward, she reported all the discourse to him. My father, after showing a great concern at it, said to her, with a sigh, "That boy might be happy if he would stay at home, but if he goes abroad, he will be the most miserable wretch that was ever born; I can give no consent to it."

It was not till almost a year after this that I broke loose, though in the meantime I continued obstinately deaf to all proposals of settling to business, and frequently expostulated with my father and mother about their being so positively determined against what they knew my inclinations prompted me to. But one day when I was at Hull, where I went casually, and without any purpose of running away that time, one of my companions who was about to sail to London in his father's ship prompted me to go with them, with the common allurement of seafaring men, that it should cost me nothing for my passage. I consulted neither father nor mother any more, nor so much as sent them word of it. Leaving them to hear of it as they might, without asking God's blessing, or my father's, without any consideration of circumstances or consequences, and in an ill hour—God knows—on the first of September, 1651, I went on board a ship bound for London. Never any young adventurer's misfortunes, I believe, began sooner, or con-

tinued longer than mine. The ship was no sooner gotten out of the Humber, but the wind began to blow, and the waves to rise in a most frightful manner. As I had never been at sea before, I was most inexpressibly sick in body and terrified in mind. I began now seriously to reflect upon what I had done, and how justly I was overtaken by the judgment of heaven for my wickedly leaving my father's house, and abandoning my duty. All the good counsel of my parents, my father's tears and my mother's entreaties, came now fresh into my mind, and my conscience, which was not yet come to the pitch of hardness to which it has been since, reproached me with the contempt of advice, and the breach of my duty to God and my father.

All this while the storm increased, and the sea, which I had never been upon before, went very high, though nothing like what I have seen many times since; no, nor like what I saw a few days after; but it was enough to affect me then, who was but a young sailor, and had never known anything of the matter. I expected that every wave would have swallowed us up, and that every time the ship fell down, as I thought, in the trough or hollow of the sea, we should never rise more. In this agony of mind I made many vows and resolutions, that if it would please God here to spare my life this one voyage, if ever I got my foot upon dry land again I would go directly home to my father, and never set it into a ship again while I lived; that I would take his advice, and never run myself into such miseries as these any more. Now I saw plainly the goodness of his observations about the middle station of life, how easy, how comfortably he had lived all his days, and never had been exposed to tempests at sea or troubles on shore. I resolved that I would, like a true repenting prodigal, go home to my father.

These wise and sober thoughts continued all the while the storm continued, and indeed some time after; but the next day the wind was abated and the sea

calmer, and I began to be a little used to it. However,
I was very grave for all that day, being also a little
seasick still, but toward night the weather cleared up,
the wind was quite over, and a charming fine evening
followed. The sun went down perfectly clear, and
rose so the next morning. There was little or no
wind, and a smooth sea with the sun shining upon it,
and the sight was, as I thought, the most delightful
that ever I saw.

I had slept well in the night, and was now no more
seasick, but very cheerful, looking with wonder upon
the sea that was so rough and terrible the day before,
and could be so calm and so pleasant in so little time
after. And now, lest my good resolutions should
continue, my companion, who had indeed enticed
me away, comes to me.

"Well, Bob," says he (clapping me upon the shoulder), "how do you do after it? I warrant you were
frighted, wan't you, last night, when it blew but a
capful of wind?"

"A capful do you call it?" said I. "It was a terrible
storm."

"A terrible storm, you silly creature?" replied he,
half laughing. "Do you call that a storm? Why, it
was nothing at all! Give us but a good ship and sea
room, and we think nothing of such a squall of wind
as that; but you're but a fresh-water sailor, Bob.
Come, let us make a bowl of punch, and we'll forget
all that. Do you see what charming weather it is
now?"

To make short this sad part of my story, we went the old way of all sailors; the punch was made, and I was made drunk with it, and in that one night's wickedness I drowned all my repentance, all my reflections upon my past conduct, and all my resolutions for my future. In a word, as the sea was returned to its smoothness of surface and settled calmness by the abatement of that storm, so the hurry of my thoughts being over, my fears and apprehensions of being swallowed up by the sea being forgotten, and the current of my former desires returned, I entirely forgot the vows and promises that I made in my distress. I found indeed some intervals of reflection, and the serious thoughts did, as it were, endeavor to return again sometimes; but I shook them off, and roused myself from them as it were from a distemper, and applying myself to drink and company, soon mastered the return of those fits, for so I called them. Thus in five or six days I had got as complete a victory over conscience as any young fellow that resolved not to be troubled with it could desire. But I was to have another trial for it still, and Providence resolved to leave me entirely without excuse. For if I would not take this for a deliverance, the next was to be such a one that the worst and most hardened wretch among us would confess both the danger and the mercy.

The sixth day of our being at sea we came into Yarmouth Roads. The wind having been contrary and the weather calm, we had made but little way since the storm. Here we were obliged to come to an anchor, and here we lay, the wind continuing contrary, namely, at southwest, for seven or eight days, during which time a great many ships from Newcastle came into the same Roads, as the common harbor where the ships might wait for a wind from the river.

We should not have ridden here so long, however, but should have gone up the river on the tide, but that the wind blew too fresh, and after we had lain four or five days blew very hard. However, the Roads being reckoned as good as a harbor, the anchorage good and our ground tackle very strong, our men were unconcerned, and not in the least apprehensive of danger, but spent the time in rest and mirth, after the manner of the sea. The eighth day in the morning the wind increased, and we had all hands at work to strike our topmasts, and make everything snug and close, that the ship might ride as easy as possible. By noon the sea went very high indeed, and our ship rode forecastle in, shipped several seas, and we thought once or twice our anchor had come home; upon which our master ordered out the sheet anchor, so that we rode with two anchors ahead, and the cables veered out to the end.

By this time it blew a terrible storm indeed, and now I began to see terror and amazement in the faces even of the seamen themselves. The master, though vigilant in the business of preserving the ship, yet as he went in and out of his cabin by me, I could hear him softly to himself several times, "Lord, be merciful

to us; we shall be all lost, we shall be all undone," and
the like. During these first hurries, I was stupid, lying
still in my cabin, which was in the steerage, and cannot describe my temper. I could ill reassume the first
penitence which I had so apparently trampled upon,
and hardened myself against. I thought the bitterness
of death had been past, and that this would be nothing
like the first. But when the master himself came by
me, as I said just now, and said we should be all lost,
I was dreadfully frightened. I got up out of my cabin
and looked out, but such a dismal sight I never saw.
The sea went mountains high, and broke upon us
every three or four minutes. When I could look
about, I could see nothing but distress round us. Two
ships that rode near us, we found, had cut their masts
by the board, being deep-laden, and our men cried
out that a ship which rode about a mile ahead of us
was foundered. Two more ships, being driven from
their anchors, were run out of the Roads to sea, and
that with not a mast standing. The light ships fared
the best, because they did not labor so much in the
sea; but two or three of them drove, and came close
by us, running away with only their spritsail out before
the wind.

Toward evening the mate and the boatswain begged
the master of our ship to let them cut away the foremast, which he was very unwilling to do; but the
boatswain protesting to him, that if he did not, the
ship would founder, he consented. When they had

cut away the foremast, the mainmast stood so loose and shook the ship so much that they were obliged to cut her away, also, and make a clear deck.

Anyone may judge what a condition I was in at all this, who was but a young sailor, and who had been in such a fright before at but a little. But if I can express at this distance the thoughts I had about me at that time, I was in tenfold more horror of mind on account of my former convictions, and because I had turned from them to the resolutions I had wickedly taken at first, than I was at death itself. These, added to the terror of the storm, put me into such a condition that I can by no words describe it.

We had a good ship, but she was deep-laden and wallowed in the sea, so that the seamen every now and then cried out that she would founder. It was my advantage in one respect that I did not know what they meant by founder, till I inquired. However, the storm was so violent that I saw what is not often seen, the master, the boatswain, and some others more sensible than the rest, at their prayers, and expecting every moment that the ship would go to the bottom. In the middle of the night, on top of all the rest of our distresses, one of the men that had been down on purpose to see, cried out that we had sprung a leak; another said there were four feet of water in the hold. Then all hands were called to the pump. At that very word my heart, as I thought, died within me, and I fell backward from the side of my bed where I sat, into the cabin.

However, the men roused me, and told me that I, who was able to do nothing before, was as well able to pump as another. At this I stirred up and went to the pump and worked very heartily. While this was doing, the master saw some light colliers, who, not able to ride out the storm, were obliged to slip and run away to sea. They would not come near us and the master ordered a gun to be fired as a signal of distress.

I, who knew nothing what that meant, was so surprised that I thought the ship had broken, or some dreadful thing happened. In a word, I was so surprised that I fell down in a swoon. As this was a time when everybody had his own life to think of, nobody minded me, or what was become of me; but another man stepped up to the pump, and thrusting me aside with his foot, let me lie, thinking I had been dead. It was a great while before I came to myself.

We worked on, but the water increasing in the hold, it was apparent that the ship would founder. Though the storm began to abate a little, yet it was not possible she could swim till we might run into a port, so the master continued firing guns for help, and a light ship who had ridden it out just ahead of us, ventured a boat out to help us. It was with the utmost hazard that the boat came near us, but it was impossible for us to get on board, or for the boat to lie near the ship's side. At last, the men rowing very heartily, and venturing their lives to save ours, our men cast them a rope over the stern with the buoy to it, and

then veered it out a great length, which they, after
great labor and hazard, took hold of, and we hauled
them close under our stern and got all into their boat.
It was to no purpose for them or us after we were in
the boat to think of reaching to their own ship, so all
agreed to let her drive, and only to pull her in toward
shore as much as we could, and our master promised
them that if the boat was staved upon shore he would
make it good to their master. So, partly rowing and
partly driving, our boat went away to the northward,
sloping toward the shore almost as far as Winterton-
Ness.

We were not much more than a quarter of an hour
out of our ship before we saw her sink, and then I
understood for the first time what was meant by a
ship foundering in the sea. I must acknowledge that
I had hardly eyes to look up when the seamen told
me she was sinking; for from that moment they rather
put me into the boat than that I might be said to go
in, my heart was, as it were, dead within me, partly
with fright, partly with horror of mind, and the
thoughts of what was yet before me.

While we were in this condition, the men yet labor-
ing at the oars to bring the boat near the shore, we
could see (when our boat mounting the waves we
were able to see the shore) a great many people running along the shore to assist us when we should come
near. We made but slow way toward the shore, nor
were we able to reach it, till being past the lighthouse
at Winterton, the shore falls off to the westward to-

ward Cromer, and so the land broke off a little the violence of the wind. Here we got in, and, though not without much difficulty, got all safe on shore, and walked afterward on foot to Yarmouth, where, as unfortunate men, we were used with great humanity, as well by the magistrate of the town, who assigned us good quarters, as by particular merchants and owners of ships, and had money given us sufficient to carry us either to London or back to Hull, as we thought fit.

But my ill fate pushed me on now with an obstinacy that nothing could resist, and though I had several times loud calls from my reason and my more composed judgment to go home, yet I had no power to do it.

My comrade, who had helped to harden me before, and who was the master's son, was now less forward than I. The first time he spoke to me after we were at Yarmouth, which was not till two or three days, for we were separated in the town to several quarters, it appeared his tone was altered. He looked very melancholy, and, shaking his head, asked me how I did. He told his father who I was, and how I had come this voyage only for a trial, in order to go farther abroad. His father turned to me with a very grave and concerned tone.

"Young man," said he, "you ought never to go to sea any more; you ought to take this for a plain and visible token that you are not to be a seafaring man."

"Why, sir," said, I "will you go to sea no more?"

"That is another case," said he. "It is my calling, and therefore my duty; but as you made this voyage for a trial, you see what a taste heaven has given you of what you are to expect if you persist; perhaps this is all befallen us on your account, like Jonah,* in the ship of Tarshish. Pray," continued he, "what are you? and on what account did you go to sea?"

I told him some of my story, at the end of which he burst out with a strange kind of passion. "What had I done," says he, "that such an unhappy wretch should come into my ship? I would not set my foot in the same ship with thee again for a thousand pounds." However, he afterward talked very gravely to me, and exhorted me to go back to my father and not tempt Providence to my ruin. He told me I might see a visible hand of heaven against me.

We parted soon after, for I made him little answer, and I saw him no more. Which way he went, I know not. As for me, having some money in my pocket, I traveled to London by land, and there, as well as on the road, had many struggles with myself, what course of life I should take, and whether I should go home, or go to sea.

---

* See Bible, Jonah 1:1–15.

Adventures In Africa ☙

I N this state of life, however, I remained some time,
uncertain what measures to take and what course
of life to lead. An irresistible reluctance continued to
going home, and as I stayed awhile, the remembrance
of the distress I had been in wore off, till at last I quite
laid aside the thoughts of it.

That evil influence which carried me first away
from my father's house, that hurried me into the wild
notion of raising my fortune, and that impressed those
conceits so forcibly upon me, as to make me deaf to
all good advice, and to the entreaties and even the
command of my father—I say, the same influence,
whatever it was, presented the most unfortunate of all
enterprises to my view, and I went on board a vessel
bound to the coast of Africa, or, as our sailors vulgarly
call it, a voyage to Guinea.

It was my great misfortune that in all these adventures I did not ship myself as a sailor; whereby, though
I might indeed have worked a little harder than ordinary, yet at the same time I should have learned the

duty and office of a foremast man, and in time might have qualified myself for a mate or a lieutenant, if not for a master. But, as it was always my fate to choose for the worse, so I did here; for having money in my pocket, and good clothes upon my back, I would always go on board in the habit of a gentleman, and so I neither had any business in the ship, nor learned to do any.

It was my lot first of all to fall into pretty good company in London, which does not always happen to such loose and unguided young fellows as I then was. I became acquainted with the master of a ship who had been on the coast of Guinea, and who, having had very good success there, was resolved to go again. He took a fancy to my conversation, and hearing me say that I had a mind to see the world, he told me that if I would go the voyage with him I should be at no expense; I should be his messmate and his companion, and if I could carry anything with me, I should have all the advantage of it that the trade would admit, and perhaps I might meet with some encouragement.

I embraced the offer, and entering into a strict friendship with this captain, who was an honest and plain-dealing man, I went the voyage with him, and undertook a small adventure in which, by the disinterested honesty of my friend the captain, I was very successful. I carried about £40* in such toys

---

* £40 = 40 pounds English money. In 1653 a pound was worth many times its present value.

and trifles as the captain directed me to buy. This
£40 I had mustered together by the assistance of some
of my relations whom I corresponded with, and who,
I believe, got my father, or at least my mother, to
contribute so much as that to my first adventure.

This was the only voyage which I may say was
successful in all my adventures, and which I owe to
the integrity and honesty of my friend the captain,
under whom also I got a complete knowledge of the
mathematics and the rules of navigation, learned how
to keep an account of the ship's course, take an observation, and, in short, to understand some things
that were needful to be understood by a sailor. As
he took delight to instruct me, I took delight to learn,
and, in a word, this voyage made me both a sailor
and a merchant, for I brought home five pounds, nine
ounces of gold dust for my adventure. This yielded
me in London at my return almost £300, and my
success filled me with those aspiring thoughts which
have since so completed my ruin.

Yet even in this voyage I had my misfortunes, too.
I was continually sick, being thrown into a violent
fever by the excessive heat of the climate. Our
principal trading was upon the coast, from the latitude of fifteen degrees north even to the line itself.

I was now set up for a Guinea trader. To my
great misfortune, my friend died soon after his ar-
rival, but I resolved to go the same voyage again. I
embarked in the same vessel with one who was the
mate in the former voyage, and had now got the

command of the ship. This was the unhappiest voyage that ever man made, for though I did not carry quite £100 of my newgained wealth, so that I had £200, left, which I lodged with my friend's widow, who was very just to me, yet I fell into terrible misfortunes in this voyage.

Our ship, making her course toward the Canary Islands, or rather between those islands and the African shore, was surprised in the gray of the morning by a Turkish rover of Sallee, who gave chase to us with all the sail she could make. We crowded, also, as much canvas as our yards would spread, or our masts carry, to have got clear, but finding that the pirate had gained upon us, and would certainly come up with us in a few hours, we prepared to fight. Our ship had twelve guns, and the rogue's eighteen. About three in the afternoon he came up with us, and bringing to, by mistake, just athwart our quarter, instead of athwart our stern, as he intended, we brought eight of our guns to bear on that side, and poured in a broadside upon him, which made him sheer off again, after returning our fire and pouring in also his small shot from about 200 men which he had on board. However, we had not a man touched, all our men keeping close. He prepared to attack us again, and we to defend ourselves, but laying us on board the next time upon our other quarter, he entered sixty men upon our decks, who immediately fell to cutting and hacking the decks and rigging. We plied them with small shot, half-pikes, powder

chests, and suchlike, and cleared our deck of them twice. However, to cut short this melancholy part of our story, our ship being disabled, and three of our men killed and eight wounded, we were obliged to yield, and were carried all prisoners into Sallee, a port belonging to the Moors.

The usage I had there was not so dreadful as at first I apprehended, nor was I carried up the country to the emperor's court, as the rest of our men were, but was kept by the captain of the rover as his proper prize, and made his slave, being young and nimble, and fit for his business. At this surpris-

ing change of my circumstances, from a merchant to
a miserable slave, I was perfectly overwhelmed, and
now I looked back upon my father's prophetic discourse to me, that I should be miserable and have
none to relieve me.

After about two years an odd circumstance presented itself, which put the old thought of making
some attempt for my liberty again in my head. My
patron lay at home longer than usual without fitting
out his ship, which, as I heard, was for want of
money. He used constantly, once or twice a week,
sometimes oftener if the weather was fair, to take
the ship's pinnace, and go out into the road fishing.
He always took me and a young Maresco* with
him to row the boat, and we made him very merry.
I proved very dexterous in catching fish, so that
sometimes he would send me with a Moor,† one of
his kinsmen, and the youth, the Maresco as they
called him, to catch a dish of fish for him.

It happened, one time, that as we went fishing in
a stark, calm morning, a fog rose so thick that,
though we were not half a league from the shore,
we lost sight of it; and rowing we knew not whither
or which way, we labored all day, and all the next
night, and when the morning came we found we
had pulled off to sea instead of pulling in for the
shore, and that we were at least two leagues from

---

* Maresco = One born on the shores of the Mediterranean Sea; more especially applied to one born on the southern shore.
 † Moor = A native of Morocco. In the Middle Ages the term was applied
to the Mohammedans who crossed over to Spain.

the shore. However, we got well in again, though
with a great deal of labor and some danger, for the
wind began to blow pretty fresh in the morning,
but particularly we were all very hungry.

But out patron, warned by this disaster, resolved
to take more care of himself in the future. He resolved that he would not go fishing any more without a compass and some provisions; so he ordered
the carpenter of his ship, who also was an English
slave, to build a little stateroom or cabin in the middle of the longboat, like that of a barge, with a place
to stand behind it to steer and hale home the main-
sheet, and room before for a hand or two to stand
and work the sails. She sailed with what we call a
shoulder-of-mutton sail; and the boom gibed over
the top of the cabin, which lay very snug and low,
and had in it room for him to lie, with a slave or two,
and a table to eat on, with some small lockers to put
his bread, rice, and coffee.

We frequently went out with this boat fishing,
and as I was most dexterous to catch fish for him, he
never went without me. It happened one time that
he had decided to go out in this boat, either for pleasure or for fish, with two or three Moors. He therefore sent on board the boat overnight a larger store
of provisions than ordinary, and had ordered me to
get ready three fusees* with powder and shot, which
were on board his ship, since he designed some sport
of fowling as well as fishing.

* A fusee was a flintlock musket. The word is now obsolete.

I got all things ready as he directed, and waited the next morning with the boat washed clean, her flag and pennants out, and everything to accommodate his guests. By and by my patron came on board alone, and told me that his guests had put off going, upon some business that fell out, and ordered me with the man and boy, as usual, to go out with the boat and catch them some fish, because his friends were to sup at his house. He commanded that as soon as I got some fish I should bring it home to his house. All this I prepared to do.

This moment my former notions of deliverance darted into my thoughts, for now I found that I was about to have a little ship at my command. As soon as my master was gone, I prepared to furnish myself, not for a fishing business, but for a voyage; though I knew not, neither did I so much as consider, whither I should steer. Anywhere to get out of that place was my way.

My first contrivance was to make a pretense to speak to this Moor, to get more food on board. I told him that we must not presume to eat of our patron's bread. He said that that was true and brought a large basket of rusks or biscuits of their kind, and three jars with fresh water, into the boat. I knew where my patron's case of bottles stood, which it was evident by the make were taken out of some English prize, and I conveyed them into the boat while the Moor was on shore, as if they had been there before for our master. I conveyed also a great

lump of beeswax into the boat, which weighed above
half a hundredweight, with a parcel of twine or
thread, a hatchet, a saw, and a hammer, all of which
were of great use to us afterward; especially the wax
to make candles.   Another trick I tried upon him
which he innocently came into also.   His name was
Ismael, but he was called Muly, or Moley, so I called
him, "Moley, our patron's guns are on board the
boat; can you not get a little powder and shot?   It
may be that we may kill some alcamies (a fowl like
our curlews) for ourselves, for I know that he keeps
the gunner's stores in the ship."

"Yes," says he, "I'll bring some."

Accordingly he brought a great leather pouch which held about a pound and a half of powder, or rather more, and another with shot, that had five or six pounds, with some bullets, and put all into the boat. At the same time I had found some powder of my master's in the great cabin, with which I filled one of the large bottles in the case, which was almost empty; pouring what was in it into another. Thus furnished with everything needful, we sailed out of the port to fish.

The men in the castle, which is at the entrance of the port, knew who we were, and took no notice of us.

We were not above a mile out of the port before we hauled in our sail and set us down to fish. The wind blew from the NNE., which was contrary to my desire, for had it blown southerly I had been sure to have made the coast of Spain, and at least reach the Bay of Cadiz; but my resolutions were, blow which way it would, I would be gone from that horrid place where I was, and leave the rest to fate.

After we had fished some time and caught nothing, for when I had fish on my hook I would not pull them up, that he might not see them, I said to the Moor, "This will not do; our master will not be thus served; we must stand farther off." He, thinking no harm, agreed, and being in the head of the boat set the sails. As I had the helm I ran the boat out nearly a league farther, and then brought her to

as if I would fish. Then, giving the boy the helm,
I stepped forward to where the Moor was, and
making as if I stooped for something behind him, I
took him by surprise with my arm under his legs,
and tossed him clear overboard into the sea. He
rose immediately, for he swam like a cork, and calling to me, begged to be taken in. He told me he
would go all over the world with me. He swam so
vigorously after the boat that he would have reached
me very quickly, there being but little wind. Thereupon I stepped into the cabin, and securing one of
the fowling pieces, I pointed it at him, and told him
that I had done him no hurt, and if he would be quiet
I would do him none.

"But," said I, "you swim well enough to reach the
shore, and the sea is calm. Make the best of your
way to shore, and I will do you no harm, but if you
come near the boat I'll shoot you through the head,
for I am resolved to have my liberty."

So he turned himself about and swam for the shore,
and I make no doubt but he reached it with ease, for
he was an excellent swimmer.

I could have been content to have taken this Moor
with me, but there was no venturing to trust him.
When he was gone I turned to the boy, whom they
called Xury, and said to him, "Xury, if you will be
faithful to me I'll make you a great man; but if you
will not stroke your face to be true to me" (that is
swear by Mahomet and his father's beard), "I must
throw you into the sea, too." The boy smiled in my

face and spoke so innocently that I could not mistrust him. He swore to be faithful to me, and go all over the world with me.

While I was in view of the Moor that was swimming, I stood out directly to sea with the boat, rather stretching to windward, that they might think me gone toward the Straits mouth (as indeed anyone that had been in his wits must have been supposed to do). Who would have supposed that we would sail on to the southward to the truly barbarian coast, where whole nations of Negroes were sure to surround us with their canoes, and destroy us; where we could never once go on shore but we should be devoured by savage beasts, or more merciless savages of human kind?

But as soon as it grew dusk in the evening, I changed my course, and steered directly south and by east, bending my course a little toward the east, that I might keep in with the shore. Having a fairly fresh gale of wind and a smooth, quiet sea, I made such sail that I believe by the next day at three o'clock in the afternoon, when I first made the land, I could not have been less than 150 miles south of Sallee. I was quite beyond the dominions of the Emperor of Morocco, or indeed of any other king thereabouts, for we saw no people.

Yet such was the fright I had taken at the Moors, and the dreadful apprehensions I had of falling into their hands, that I would not stop, or go on shore, or come to an anchor. The wind continued fair till

I had sailed in that manner five days. When it shifted to the southward, I concluded that if any of our vessels were in chase of me, they also would now give up, so I ventured to make the coast. I came to an anchor in the mouth of a little river, I knew not what, or where; neither what latitude, what country, what nation, or what river. I neither saw, nor desired to see, any people. The principal thing I wanted was fresh water. We came into this creek in the evening, resolving to swim to shore as soon as it was dark, and explore the country; but as soon as it was quite dark, we heard such dreadful noises of the barking, roaring, and howling of wild creatures of we knew not what kinds, that the poor boy was ready to die with fear, and begged me not to go on shore till day.

"Oh, very well," said I, "then I won't, but it may be that we may see men by day, who will be as bad to us as those lions."

"Then we give them the shoot gun," says Xury, laughing; "make them run away."

Such English Xury spoke by conversing among us slaves. However I was glad to see the boy so cheerful, and I gave him a dram (out of our patron's case of bottles) to cheer him up. After all, Xury's advice was good, and I took it. We dropped our little anchor and lay still all night. I say "lay still," for we slept none, for in two or three hours we saw vast, great creatures (we knew not what to call them) of many sorts, come down to the seashore and run into the water, wallowing and washing themselves for the pleasure of cooling themselves. They made such hideous howlings and yellings that I never indeed heard the like.

How to venture on shore when day came was another question, too, for to have fallen into the hands of any of the savages, had been as bad as to have fallen prey to lions and tigers; at least we were equally apprehensive of the danger of it. Be that as it would, we were obliged to go on shore somewhere or other for water, for we had not a pint left in the boat. When or where to get it was the point. Xury said that if I would let him go on shore with one of the jars he would see if there was any water, and bring some to me. I asked him why he would go; why I should not go, and he stay in the boat.

The boy answered with so much affection that I loved him ever after. Said he, "If wild mans come, they eat me, you go way."

"Well, Xury," said I, "we will both go, and if the wild mans come, we will kill them; they shall eat neither of us."

I gave Xury a piece of rusk-bread to eat, and a dram out of our patron's case of bottles which I mentioned before. Then we hauled the boat in as near the shore as we thought was proper, and waded to shore, carrying nothing but our guns, and two jars for water.

I did not care to go out of sight of the boat, fearing the coming of canoes with savages down the river; but the boy, seeing a low place about a mile up the country, rambled to it. By and by I saw him come running toward me. I thought that he was pursued by some savage, or frightened by some wild beast, and I ran forward toward him to help him, but when I came nearer to him, I saw something hanging over his shoulders. It was a creature that he had shot, like a hare, but different in color, and with longer legs. We were very glad of it, and it was very good meat. However, the great joy that poor Xury came with was to tell me that he had found good water, and had seen no wild men.

But we found afterward that we need not take such pains for water, for a little higher up the creek where we were, we found the water fresh when the tide was out, which flowed but a little way up. We filled our jars and feasted on the hare we had killed, and prepared to go on our way, having seen no footsteps of any human creature in that part of the country.

As I had been one voyage to this coast before, I knew very well that the islands of the Canaries, and the Cape Verde Islands, also, lay not far off from the coast. But as I had no instruments to take an observation to know what latitude we were in, and did not exactly know, or at least remember, what latitude they were in, I knew not where to look for them, or when to stand off to sea toward them. Otherwise I might now easily have found some of these islands. But my hope was that if I stood along this coast till I came to that part where the English traded, I should find some of their vessels upon their usual design of trade, that would relieve and take us in.

By the best of my calculation, that place where I now was must be that country which lies between the Emperor of Morocco's dominions and the Negroes, and is waste and uninhabited except by wild beasts.

Once or twice in the daytime I thought I saw the Peak of Teneriffe, which is the high top of the mountain Teneriffe in the Canaries. I had a great mind to venture out in hopes of reaching it, but having tried twice, I was forced in again by contrary winds, the sea also going too high for my little vessel, so I resolved to pursue my first design and keep along the shore.

Several times I was obliged to land for fresh water after we had left this place. Once in particular, early in the morning, we came to anchor under a little point of land and saw a great lion quietly taking his rest.

I took the best aim I could and shot him in the head, and had the pleasure to see him drop, struggling for life.

I bethought myself that perhaps the skin of him might one way or other be of some value to us, and I resolved to take off his skin, if I could. So Xury and I went to work with him; but Xury was much the better workman at it, for I knew very ill how to do it. Indeed, it took us both the whole day, but at last we got the hide off him, and spread it on the top of our cabin, where the sun effectually dried it in two days. Afterward it served me to lie upon.

After this stop, we made on to the southward continually for ten or twelve days, living very sparingly on our provisions, which began to abate very much, and going no oftener into the shore than we were obliged to for fresh water. My design in this was to make the river Gambia or Senegal, that is to say anywhere about Cape Verde, where I was in hopes to meet with some European ship. If I did not, I knew not what course I had to take but to seek for the islands, or perish there among the Negroes. I knew that all the ships from Europe, which sailed either to the coast of Guinea or to Brazil or to the East Indies, made this cape, or those islands. In a word, I put the whole of my fortune upon this single point, either that I must meet with some ship or must perish.

When I had pursued this resolution about ten days longer, as I have said, I began to see that the land was inhabited. In two or three places, as we sailed by, we saw people stand upon the shore to look at us; we could also perceive that they were quite black, and stark naked. I was once inclined to have gone on shore to them; but Xury was my better counselor, and said to me, "No go, no go." However, I hauled in nearer the shore that I might talk to them, and I found that they ran along the shore by me a good way. I observed that only one had a weapon, a long, slender stick, which Xury said was a lance. He told me that savages could throw these lances a great way with good aim. So I kept at a distance, but talked with them by signs as well as I could, and particularly made signs for something to eat. They beckoned to me to stop my boat, and they would bring me some meat. Upon this I lowered the top of my sail and lay by, and two of them ran up into the country, and in less than half an hour came back, bringing with them two pieces of dry flesh and some grain, which is the produce of their country. We neither knew what the one nor the other was, but we were willing to accept it. How to come at it was our next dispute, for I was not for venturing on shore to them, and they were as much afraid of us. However, they took a safe way for us all, for they brought it to the shore and laid it down, and went and stood a great way off till we had brought it on board. Then they came close to us again.

We made signs of thanks to them, for we had nothing to make them amends, but an opportunity offered that very instant to oblige them wonderfully. While we were lying by the shore, there came two mighty creatures, one pursuing the other (as we took it) with great fury, from the mountains toward the sea. We found the people terribly frightened, especially the women. The man that had the lance or dart did not fly from them, but the rest did. However, the two creatures did not seem to offer to fall upon any of the Negroes, but plunged themselves into the sea, and swam about as if they had come for their diversion. At last one of them be-

gan to come nearer our boat than at first I expected, but I lay ready for him, for I had loaded my gun with all possible expedition, and bade Xury load both the others. As soon as he came fairly within my reach, I fired, and shot him directly in the head. Immediately he sank down into the water, but rose instantly, and plunged up and down as if he was struggling for life, and so indeed he was. He immediately made to the shore, but between the wound which was his mortal hurt, and the strangling of the water, he died just before he reached the shore.

It is impossible to express the astonishment of these

poor Negroes at the noise and the fire of my gun. But
when they saw that the creature was dead, and sunk in
the water, and that I made signs to them to come to
the shore, they took heart and came to the shore, and
began to search for the creature. I found him by his
blood staining the water. By the help of a rope,
which I slung round him, and gave the Negroes to
haul, they dragged him on shore, and found that he
was a most curious leopard, spotted and fine to an ad-
mirable degree. The Negroes held up their hands
with admiration to think what it was that I had killed
him with.

The other creature, frightened with the flash of
fire and the noise of the gun, swam to shore, and ran
up directly to the mountains from whence they had
come, nor could I at that distance know what he was.
I quickly found that the Negroes were for eating the
flesh of this creature, so I was willing to have them
take it as a favor from me. They offered me some of
the flesh, which I declined, making as if I would give
it to them, but I made signs for the skin, which they
gave me very freely. They brought me, too, a great
deal more of their provision, which, though I did not
understand, yet I accepted. Then I made signs to
them for some water, and held out one of my jars to
them, turning it bottom upward, to show that it was
empty, and that I wanted to have it filled. They called
immediately to some of their friends, and two women
came and brought a great vessel made of earth and
burnt, as I suppose, in the sun. This they sat down

for me, as before, and I sent Xury on shore with my jars, and filled them all three.

I was now furnished with roots and grain, such as it was, and water; and, leaving my friendly Negroes, I made forward for about eleven days more, without offering to go near the shore, till I saw the land run out a great length into the sea, at about the distance of four or five leagues before me. The sea being very calm, I kept a large offing to make this point. At length, doubling the point at about two leagues from the land, I saw plainly land on the other side to seaward. Then I concluded, as it was most certain indeed, that this was Cape Verde, and those the islands, called from thence Cape Verde Islands. However, they were at a great distance, and I could not tell what I had best do, for if I should be taken with a fresh of wind I might reach neither one nor the other.

Not knowing what to do in this dilemma, I went into the cabin and sat down to think. Xury had the helm, and suddenly he cried out, "Master, master, a ship with a sail!" I jumped out of the cabin, and immediately saw the ship, and saw that it was a Portuguese ship, and, as I thought, was bound to the coast of Guinea for Negroes. But when I observed the course she steered, I was soon convinced that they were bound some other way, and did not design to come any nearer to the shore. Thereupon I stretched out to sea as much as I could, resolving to speak with them if possible.

With all the sail I could make, I found I should not

be able to come in their way, but they would be gone by before I could make any signal to them. But after I had crowded to the utmost, and began to despair, they, it seemed, saw me by the help of their perspective glasses.* They saw that it was some European boat, which, as they supposed, must belong to some ship that was lost; so they shortened sail to let me come up. I was encouraged with this, and as I had my patron's flag on board, I made a waft of it to them for a signal of distress, and fired a gun, both of which they saw, for they told me they saw the smoke, though they did not hear the gun. Upon these signals they very kindly brought to, and lay by for me, and in about three hours' time I came up with them.

They asked me what I was, in Portuguese, in Spanish, and in French, but I understood none of them. At last a Scottish sailor, who was on board, called to me, and I answered him, and told him that I was an Englishman, and that I had made my escape out of slavery from the Moors at Sallee. Then they bade me come on board, and very kindly took me in, and all my goods.

It was inexpressible joy to me, more than anyone would believe, that I was thus delivered, as I esteemed it, from such a miserable and almost hopeless condition as I was in. I immediately offered all I had to the captain of the ship, as a return for my deliverance; but he generously told me he would take nothing

---

* Perspective glasses = spyglasses = telescopes.

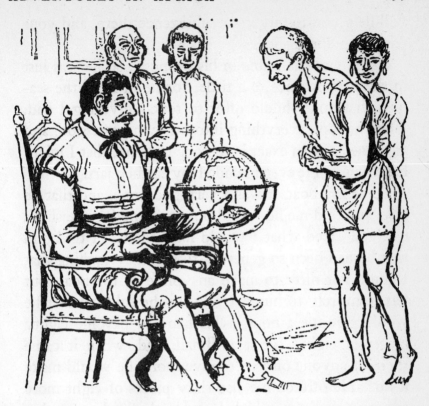

from me. He assured me that all that I had should be delivered safe to me when I came to the Brazils.

"For," said he, "I have saved your life on no other terms than I would be glad to be saved myself. It may one time or other be my lot to be taken up in the same condition. Besides," said he, "when I carry you to the Brazils, so great a way from your own country, if I should take away from you what you have, you will be starved there, and then I only take away that life I have given. No, no, Seignor, Mr. Englishman, I will carry you thither in charity, and those things

will help you to buy your subsistence there, and your
passage home again."

As he was charitable in his proposal, so he was just
in the performance to a tittle, for he ordered the seamen that none should offer to touch anything I had.
Then he took everything into his own possession, and
gave me back an exact inventory of them, that I might
have them. He even included my earthen jars.

As to my boat, it was a very good one, and that he
saw, and told me he would buy it of me for the ship's
use, and asked what I would have for it. I told him
that he had been so generous to me in everything that
I could not offer to make any price of the boat, but
left it entirely to him. Upon this he told me that he
would give me a note of his hand to pay me eighty
pieces of eight* for it at Brazil, and, when it came
there, if anyone offered to give more, he would make
it up. He offered me also sixty pieces of eight more
for my boy Xury, which I was loath to take, not that
I was not willing to let the captain have him, but I was
very loath to sell the poor boy's liberty, since he had
assisted me so faithfully in procuring my own. However, when I let the captain know my reason, he
owned it to be just, and offered me this compromise
that he would promise to set the boy free in ten years,
if he turned Christian. Upon this, when Xury said he
was willing to go to him, I let the captain have him.

---

* The piece of eight was the Spanish dollar.

Life and Travel In South America

W<small>E</small> had a very good voyage to the Brazils, and arrived in All Saints Bay in about twenty-two days. And now I was once more delivered from the most miserable of all conditions of life, and what to do next with myself I was now to consider.

The generous treatment the captain gave me I can never enough remember. He would take nothing of me for my passage, gave me twenty ducats* for the leopard's skin, and forty for the lion's skin, which I had in my boat, and caused everything I had in the ship to be punctually delivered me; and what I was willing to sell he bought, such as the case of bottles, two of my guns, and a piece of the lump of beeswax, for I had made candles of the rest. In a word, I made about two hundred and twenty pieces of eight of all my cargo, and with this stock I went on shore in the Brazils.

---

*A ducat was formerly a gold or silver European coin varying in value from about 83 cents to $2.25.

I had not been long here before I was recommended to the house of a good honest man like myself, who had an ingenio, as they call it, that is, a plantation and a sugarhouse. I lived with him some time, and acquainted myself by that means with the manner of their planting and making of sugar. Seeing how well the planters lived, and how they grew rich quickly, I resolved, if I could get license to settle there, that I would turn planter among them. I decided in the meantime to find some way to have my money, which I had left in London, remitted to me. To this purpose, getting a kind of letter of naturalization, I purchased as much land that was uncured as my money would reach, and formed a plan for my plantation and settlement, and such a one as might be suitable to the stock which I planned to receive from England.

I had a neighbor, a Portuguese of Lisbon, born of English parents, whose name was Wells. He was in much such circumstances as I was. I call him neighbor, because his plantation lay next to mine and we went on very sociably together. My stock was low, as his was, and we rather planted for food than anything else, for about two years. However, we began to increase, and our land began to come into order, so that the third we planted some tobacco, and made each of a large piece of ground ready for planting canes in the year to come; but we both wanted help.

I had no remedy but to go on; I had fallen into an employment quite remote to my genius and directly contrary to my desires. I regretted that I had left my father's house, and broken through all his good advice. I said to myself that I might as well have stayed at home in England among my friends. I ought never to have come these five thousand miles to be among strangers.

In this manner I used to look upon my condition with the utmost regret. I had nobody to converse with, but now and then this neighbor; no work to be done, but by the labor of my hands; and I used to say that I lived just like a man cast away upon some desolate island, that had nobody there but himself.

I was in some degree settled in my measures for carrying on the plantation before my kind friend, the captain of the ship that took me up at sea, went back; for the ship remained there, providing his loading and preparing for his voyage, nearly three months. When I told him what little stock I had left behind me in London, he gave me this friendly and sincere advice.

"Seignor Inglese," says he (for so he always called me), "if you will give me letters, and an order made out to me, with directions to the person who has your money in London, to send your effects to Lisbon, to such persons as I shall direct, and in such goods as are proper for this country, I will bring you the produce of them, God willing, at my return. However, since human affairs are all subject to changes and disasters, I would have you give orders for but one hundred pounds sterling, which you say is half your stock, and let the hazard be run for the first. Then, if it comes safe, you may order the rest the same way. If it miscarries, you may have the other half to have recourse to it for your supply."

This was such wholesome advice, and looked so friendly, that I could not but be convinced that it was the best course that I could take; so I accordingly prepared letters to the gentlewoman with whom I had left my money, and gave an order to the Portuguese captain, as he desired.

I wrote the English captain's widow a full account of all my adventures, my slavery, my escape, and how I had met with the Portuguese captain at sea, the humanity of his behavior, and what condition I was now in, with all other necessary directions for my supply. When this honest captain came to Lisbon, he found means, by some of the English merchants there, to send over, not the order only, but a full account of my story, to a merchant at London, who repeated it to my friend. Thereupon, she not only delivered the money, but out of her own pocket sent the Portugal captain a very handsome present for his humanity and charity to me.

The merchant in London spent this hundred pounds for English goods, such as the captain had written for, and sent them directly to him at Lisbon. He brought them all safe to me to the Brazils. Among them, without my directions (for I was too young in my business to think of them), he had taken care to have all sorts of tools, ironwork, and utensils necessary for my plantation, and which were of great use to me.

When this cargo arrived I thought my fortune

made, for I was surprised and delighted at it. My good steward the captain had taken the five pounds which my friend had sent him for a present for himself, to purchase and bring me over a servant under bond for six years' service. He would not accept any consideration, except a little tobacco of my own produce, which I insisted that he accept.

Neither was this all. My goods being all English manufactures, such as cloth, stuffs, baize, and things particularly valuable and desirable in the country, I found means to sell them to a very great advantage, so that I may say I had more than four times the value of my first cargo, and was now infinitely beyond my poor neighbor in the advancement of my plantation. The first thing I did was to buy a Negro slave and another European servant besides the one which the captain had brought me from Lisbon.

But as abused prosperity is oftentimes made the very means of our greatest adversity, so it was with me. I went on the next year with great success in my plantation. I raised fifty great rolls of tobacco on my own ground, more than I had disposed of for necessaries among my neighbors, and these fifty rolls, each above a hundredweight, were well cured and laid by against the return of the fleet from Lisbon. And now, as I increased in business and in wealth, my head began to be full of projects and undertakings beyond my reach, such as are indeed often the ruin of the best heads in business.

As I had persisted in breaking away from my par-

ents, so I could not be content now, but I must go
and leave the happy view I had of being a rich and
thriving man in my new plantation, only to pursue
a rash and immoderate desire of rising faster than the
nature of the thing admitted. Thus I cast myself
down again into the deepest gulf of human misery that
ever man fell into, or perhaps that could be consistent
with life and a state of health in the worlds.

Let me come then by the proper degrees to the
particulars of this part of my story. As you may
suppose, since I had now lived almost four years in
the Brazils, and had begun to thrive and prosper very
well upon my plantation, I had not only learned the
language, but had contracted acquaintance and friendship among my fellow planters, as well as among the
merchants at St. Salvadore, which was our port. In
my discourses among them I had frequently given
them an account of my two voyages to the coast of
Guinea, the manner of trading with the Negroes there,
and how easy it was to purchase upon the coast, for
trifles, such as beads, toys, knives, scissors, hatchets,
bits of glass, and the like, not only gold dust, Guinea
grains, elephants' teeth, but Negroes for the service of
the Brazils, in great numbers.

They listened always very attentively to my discourses on this subject, but especially to that part
which related to buying Negroes.

It happened one day that I was with some merchants
and planters of my acquaintance, and as usual I talked
of those things very earnestly. The next morning

three of them came to me and told me that they had
been thinking very much about what I had told them
the night before. They came to make a secret proposal to me, and, after enjoining secrecy, they told
me that they had a mind to fit out a ship to go to
Guinea. They all had plantations as well as I, and
were in need of servants. They knew that this was a
trade that could not be carried on indefinitely, because they could not publicly sell the Negroes when
they came home, so they desired to make but one
voyage, to bring the Negroes on shore privately, and
divide them among their own plantations. In a word,

the question was whether I would go as their super-
cargo in the ship, to manage the trading part upon the
coast of Guinea. They offered me an equal share of
the Negroes, without my providing any part of the
stock.

This would have been a fair proposal, it must be
confessed, had it been made to anyone that had not
had a settlement and plantation of his own to look
after, which was in a fair way of becoming very considerable, and with a good stock upon it. But I was
thus entered and established, and had nothing to do but
go on as I had begun, and by sending for the other
hundred pounds from England, in three or four years
I could scarcely have failed being worth three or four
thousand pounds sterling, and that increasing, too.
For me to think of such a voyage as these men proposed was the most preposterous thing that ever man
in such circumstances could be guilty of.

However, I told them that I would go with all my
heart, if they would undertake to look after my plantation in my absence, and would dispose of it to such
as I should direct if my plans miscarried. This they
all agreed to do, and entered into writing or covenants
to do so. I made a formal will, disposing of my plantation and effects, in case of my death, making the
captain of the ship that saved my life, as before, my
only heir. However, I obliged him to dispose of my
effects as I had directed in my will, one-half of the
produce being to himself, and the other to be shipped
to England.

In short, I took all possible caution to preserve my effects and keep up my plantation. Had I used half as much prudence in looking into my own interest, and making a judgment of what I ought to have done and ought not to have done, I had certainly never gone away from so prosperous an undertaking, leaving what was in all probability a thriving circumstance, to go upon a voyage to sea, attended with all its common hazards.

But I was hurried on, and obeyed blindly the dictates of my fancy rather than my reason. Accordingly, when the ship was fitted out, and the cargo furnished, and all things done as by agreement by my partners in the voyage, I went on board in an evil hour, the 1st of September—just eight years from the day when I had left my father and mother and had sailed from Hull.

Our ship was about 120 tons burden, carried 6 guns and 14 men, besides the master, his boy, and myself. We had on board no large cargo of goods, except such toys as were fit for our trade with the Negroes, such as beads, bits of glass, shells, and odd trifles, especially little looking glasses, knives, scissors, hatchet, and the like.

The same day I went on board we set sail, standing away to the northward upon our own coast, with design to stretch over for the African coast when we came about ten or twelve degrees of northern latitude, which it seems was the manner of the course in those days. We had very good weather, only excessively hot, all the way upon our own coast till we came to height of Cape St. Augustino; from there, keeping farther off at sea, we lost sight of land, and steered as if we were bound for the isle Fernando de Noronha, holding our course NE. by N. and leaving those isles on the east. In this course we passed the line in about twelve days' time, and were by our last observation in seven degrees twenty-two minutes northern latitude, when a violent tornado or hurricane took us quite out of our knowledge. It began from the southeast, came about to the northwest, and then settled into the northeast, whence it blew in such a terrible manner, that for twelve days together we could do nothing but drive, and scudding away before it, let it carry us wherever fate and the fury of the winds directed.

In this distress, besides the terror of the storm, one of our men died of fever, and one man and the boy were washed overboard. About the twelfth day when the weather abated a little, the master made an observation as well as he could, and found that he was in about eleven degrees north latitude, but that he was twenty-two degrees of longitude difference west from Cape St. Augustino. Thus he found that he was off the north coast of Brazil, beyond the river Amazones,* toward that of the river Oronoque,* commonly called the Great River.

I studied the charts with him, and we concluded

---

* The Amazones is the Amazon, and the Oronoque the Orinoco.

that there was no inhabited country where we could land, till we came within the circle of the Caribbee Islands. Therefore we resolved to stand away for Barbados, which, by keeping off at sea to avoid the current of the bay or Gulf of Mexico, we could easily reach, as we hoped, in about fifteen days' sail. On the other hand, we could not possibly make our voyage to the coast of Africa without some assistance, both to our ship and to ourselves.

With this design we changed our course, and steered away NW. by W. in order to reach some of our English islands, where I hoped for relief. However, our voyage was otherwise determined. When we were in the latitude of twelve degrees eighteen minutes, a second storm came upon us, which carried us westward with the same force and drove us so out of the way of civilization, that had all our lives been saved, as to the sea, we were in danger of being devoured by savages.

While we were in this distress with the wind still blowing very hard, one of our men early in the morning cried out, "Land!" We had no sooner ran out of the cabin to look out, in the hope of seeing where in the world we were, when the ship struck upon sand, and in a moment, the sea broke over her in such a manner that we expected to perish immediately. We were driven at once into our close quarters for shelter from the very foam and spray of the sea.

It is not easy for anyone who has not been in the

same condition to conceive the consternation of men in such circumstances. We knew nothing where we were, or upon what land it was we were driven, whether an island or the main, whether inhabited or not inhabited. As the rage of the wind was still great, though rather less than at first, we could not so much as hope to have the ship hold many minutes without breaking in pieces, unless the winds, by a kind of miracle, should turn immediately about. In a word, we sat looking one upon another, and expecting death every moment. Every man acted accordingly as though he were preparing for another world, for there was little or nothing more for us to do in this. Our present comfort, and all the comfort we had, was that, contrary to our expectation, the ship did not break yet, and the master said the wind began to abate.

Now, though we found that the wind did a little abate, yet the ship was sticking too fast upon the sand for us to expect to get her off, and we were in a dreadful condition indeed. We had nothing to do but think of saving our lives as well as we could. We had a boat on board, but how to get off into the sea was a doubtful thing. However, there was no time to debate, for we fancied the ship would break in pieces every minute, and some told us she was actually beginning to break already.

In this distress, the mate of our vessel lay hold of the boat, and with the help of the rest of the men, got her slung over the ship's side. We all, eleven in number, got into her, let go, and committed ourselves to God's mercy and the wild sea.

And now our case was very dismal indeed, for we all saw plainly that the sea went so high that the boat could not live, and that we should be inevitably drowned. We had no sail, nor, if we had, could we have done anything with it, so we worked at the oar toward the land, though with heavy hearts, like men going to execution. We all knew that when the boat came nearer the shore she would be dashed in a thousand pieces by the breach of the sea. However, we committed our souls to God in the most earnest manner, and the wind driving us toward the shore, we hastened our destruction with our own hands, pulling as well as we could toward land.

What the shore was, whether rock or sand, whether steep or shoal, we knew not. The only hope that could rationally give us the least shadow of expectation was that we might happen into some bay or gulf, or the mouth of some river, where by great chance we could run our boat in, or get under the lee of the land, and perhaps make smooth water. But nothing of this kind appeared, and as we made nearer and nearer the shore, the land looked more frightful than the sea.

After we had rowed, or rather driven, about a league and a half, as we reckoned it, a raging wave, mountain-like, came rolling astern of us. It took us with such a fury that it upset the boat at once, and separated us, as well from the boat as from one another.

Nothing can describe the confusion of thought which I felt when I sank into the water. Although I swam very well, I could not deliver myself from the water so as to draw breath, till that wave, having driven me, or rather carried me, a vast way on toward the shore, spent itself, and went back, leaving me upon the land almost dry, but half-dead with the water I took in. I had so much presence of mind, as well as breath left, that, seeing myself nearer the mainland than I expected, I got upon my feet, and endeavored to make on toward it as fast as I could, before another wave should return and take me up again. But I soon found that it was impossible to avoid it. I saw the sea come after me as high as a great hill, and as furious as an enemy which I had no means or strength to contend with. My business was to hold my breath, and raise myself upon the water, if I could, and pilot myself toward safety if possible. My greatest concern now was that the wave that would carry me a great way toward the shore when it came on, might not carry me back again with it when it gave back toward the sea.

The wave that came upon me again buried me at once twenty or thirty feet deep in its own body, and I could feel myself carried with a might force and swiftness toward the shore a very great way. I held my breath, and assisted myself to swim forward with all my might. I was ready to burst with holding my breath, when I felt myself rising up, and to my immediate relief, I found my head and hands shoot out above the surface of the water. Though it was not two seconds of time that I could keep myself so, yet it relieved me greatly, gave me breath and new courage. I was covered again with water a good while, but not so long but I held it out. When I found that the water had spent itself and was beginning to return, I struck forward against the return of the waves, and felt ground again with my feet. I stood still a few moments to recover breath, and till the water went from me, and then took to my heels and ran with what strength I had farther up the shore. But neither would this deliver me from the fury of the sea, which came pouring in after me again, and twice more I was lifted up by the waves and carried forward as before, the shore being very flat.

The last time was almost fatal to me, for it dashed me against a piece of rock with such force that it left me senseless, and helpless to save myself. I struck my side and breast, so that the breath was beaten out of my body, and had it not returned again immediately, I must have been strangled in the water. However, I recovered a little before the return of the waves, and since the waves were not so high as at first, being near land, I held fast to the rock till the wave abated. Then I managed another run, which brought me so near the shore that the next wave, though it went over me, did

not carry me away.   The next run I took I got to the
mainland, where, to my great comfort, I clambered
up the clefts of the shore, and sat down upon the grass,
free from danger, and quite out of the reach of the
water.

Salvage from the Wreck ❧

I was now landed and safe on shore, and began to
look up and thank God that my life was saved,
when some minutes before there had been scarcely any
room to hope. I believe it is impossible to express in
full what the ecstasies and transports of the soul are,
when it is so saved, as I may say, out of the very grave.
I walked about on the shore, lifting up my hands, and
my whole being, wrapped up in the contemplation of
my deliverance, reflecting upon all my comrades that
were drowned, for I never saw them afterward, or any
sign of them, except three of their hats, one cap, and
two shoes that were not fellows.

I cast my eyes to the stranded vessel, when the
breach and froth of the sea being so big, I could hardly
see it, it lay so far off, and wondered how it was possible that I had reached shore!

After I had solaced my mind with the comfortable
part of my condition, I began to look around me, to
see what kind of place I was in, and what was next to
be done. I soon found that I had had a dreadful de-

liverance. For I was wet, and had no clothes to change to, nor anything either to eat or drink to comfort me. Moreover, I saw no prospect before me but that of perishing with hunger, or of being devoured by wild beasts. I was particularly disturbed because I had no weapon either to hunt and kill any creature for my sustenance, or to defend myself against any other creature that might desire to kill me for his. In a word, I had nothing about me but a knife, a tobacco pipe, and a little tobacco in a box. This threw me into such terrible agonies of mind that for a while I ran about like a madman. When night came upon me, I began with a heavy heart to consider what would be my lot if there were any ravenous beasts in that country, since at night they always come abroad for their prey.

The only thing that I could think of to do was to climb up into a thick, bushy tree like a fir, although it was thorny, which grew near me. I resolved to sit there all night, and consider the next day what death I should die, for as yet I saw no prospect of life. I walked about a furlong from the shore, to see if I could find any fresh water to drink, which I did, to my great joy. When I had drunk, and put a little tobacco in my mouth to prevent hunger, I went to the tree, and climbing up into it tried to place myself so as that if I should sleep I might not fall. When I had cut a short stick for my defense, I settled myself and, since I was extremely tired, fell fast asleep, and slept comfortably as, I believe, few could have done in my condition.

When I waked it was broad day, the weather clear and the storm abated, so that the sea did not rage and swell as before. What surprised me most, however, was that the ship had been lifted by the swelling tide from the sand where she had lain and was driven up almost as far as the rock against which I had been dashed. This was within about a mile from the shore where I was, and since the ship seemed to stand upright still, I wished myself on board, that, at least, I might save some necessary things for my use.

When I came down from my apartment in the tree, I looked about me again, and the first thing I found was the boat, which lay as the wind and the sea had tossed her, up upon the land, about two miles on my right hand. I walked along the shore to reach her, but found a neck or inlet of water about half a mile broad between me and the boat; so I came back for the present, being more intent upon getting at the ship, where I hoped to find some food.

A little after noon I found the sea very calm, and the tide ebbed so far out that I could come within a quarter of a mile of the ship, and here I found a fresh renewing of my grief. I saw that if we had kept on board, we should all have reached shore in safety and I should not have been so miserable as to be left entirely destitute of all comfort and company, as I now was. This forced tears from my eyes again, but as there was little relief in that, I resolved, if possible, to get to the ship. I pulled off my clothes, for the weather was hot to extremity, and took the water. When I came to the ship, my difficulty was still greater to know how to get on board, for as she lay aground, and high out of the water, there was nothing within my reach to lay hold of. I swam round her twice, and the second time I spied a small piece of rope, which I wondered I had not seen at first. It hung down by the forechains so low that with great difficulty I got hold of it, and by the help of that rope got up into the forecastle of the ship. Here I found that the ship was bulged and had a great deal of water in her hold, but that she lay so on the side of a bank of hard sand, or rather earth, that her stern lay lifted up upon the bank, and her head low almost to the water. By this means all her quarter was free, and all that was in that part was dry. You may be sure my first work was to search to see what was spoiled and what was free. First I found that all the ship's provisions were dry and untouched by the water, and being very hungry, I went to the bread room and filled my pockets with biscuits, and ate them as I went about other things, for I had no time to lose. Now I wanted nothing but a boat to furnish myself with many things which I foresaw would be very necessary to me.

It was in vain to sit still and wish for what was not to be had, and this extremity roused my application. We had several spare yards, and two or three large spars of wood, and a spare topmast or two in the ship.

I resolved to fall to work with these, and flung as many of them overboard as I could manage for their weight, tying every one with a rope to form a raft.

My raft was now strong enough for any reasonable weight. My next care was what to load it with, and how to preserve what I laid upon it from the surf of the sea, but I was not long considering this. I first laid all the planks or boards upon it that I could get, and having considered well what I most wanted, I got three of the seamen's chests, which I had broken open and emptied, and lowered them down upon my raft. The first of these I filled with provisions, bread, rice, three Dutch cheeses, five pieces of dried goat's flesh, which we lived much upon, and a little remainder of European grain. There had been some barley and wheat together, but, to my great disappointment, I found afterward that the rats had eaten or spoiled it all. As for liquors, I found several cases of bottles belonging to our skipper, in which were some cordial waters, and in all about five or six gallons. These I stowed by themselves, there being no need to put them into the chest and no room for them. While I was doing this, I found that the tide had begun to flow, though very calmly, and I had the mortification of seeing my coat, shirt, and waistcoat, which I had left on shore upon the sand, swim away. My breeches were only linen and open-kneed, and I had swum on board in them and my stockings. However, this set me to rummaging for clothes, of which I found enough, but took no more than I wanted for present use. I had other things which my eye was more upon, such as tools to work with on shore. It was after long searching that I found the carpenter's chest, which was indeed a very useful prize to me, and much more valuable than a shipload of gold would have been at that time. I got it down to my raft, even whole as it was, without losing time to look into it, for I knew in general what it contained.

My next care was for some ammunition and arms. There were two very good fowling pieces in the great cabin and two pistols. These I secured first, with some powder horns, and a small bag of shot and two old rusty swords. I knew that there were three barrels of powder in the ship, but knew not where our gunner had stowed them. After much search I found them, two of them dry and good, but the third had taken water. Those two I got to my raft, with the arms. Now I thought myself pretty well freighted, and began to wonder how I should get to shore with them, having neither sail, oar, nor rudder, and the least cupful of wind would have upset all my navigation.

I had three encouragements: a smooth, calm sea, the tide rising and setting into the shore, and what little wind there was blowing me toward the land. Thus having found two or three broken oars belonging to the boat, and besides the tools which were in the chest, I found two saws, an ax, and a hammer, and with this cargo I put to sea. For a mile, or thereabouts, my raft went very well, except that I found it to drive a

little distant from the place where I had landed before, by which I perceived that there was some current of the water, and consequently I hoped to find some creek or river there, which I might make use of as a port to get to land with my cargo.

At length I spied a little cove on the right shore of the creek, to which, with great pain and difficulty, I guided my raft, and at last got so near, that, reaching ground with my oar, I could thrust her directly in. But here I almost dipped all my cargo in the sea again, for that shore sloped, so that there was no place to land, except where one end of the float, if it ran on shore, would lie so high, and the other sink so low, that it would endanger my cargo. All that I could do was to wait till the tide was at the highest, keeping the raft with my oar like an anchor to hold the side of it fast to the shore, near a flat piece of ground, which I expected the water would flow over, and so it did. As soon as I found water enough (for my raft drew about a foot of water), I thrust her upon that flat piece of ground, and there fastened or moored her by sticking my two broken oars into the ground, one on one side near one end, and one on the other side near the other end. Thus I lay till the water ebbed away, and left my raft and all my cargo safe on shore.

My next work was to view the country, and seek a proper place for my dwelling, and a place to stow my goods to secure them from whatever might happen. Where I was I yet knew not; whether on the continent or on an island, whether surrounded by savages or alone, whether in danger of wild beasts or not. There was a hill not more than a mile from me, which rose up very steep and high, and which seemed to overtop some other hills which lay as in a ridge from it northward. I took out one of the fowling pieces, and one of the pistols, and a horn of powder, and thus armed I traveled up to the top of that hill to look over the ground. There, after I had with great labor and difficulty reached the top, I saw my fate. I was in an island surrounded on all sides by the sea. There was no land to be seen, except some rocks which lay a great way off, and two small islands less than this, which lay about three leagues to the west.

I found also that the island I was in was barren, and, as I saw good reason to believe, uninhabited, except by wild beasts, of whom, however, I saw none. I saw

abundance of fowls, but knew not their kinds, neither when I killed them could I tell what was fit for food, and what not. On my way back I shot at a great bird, which I saw sitting upon a tree on the side of a wood. I believe it was the first gun that had ever been fired there. I had no sooner fired than from all parts of the wood there arose an innumerable number of fowls of many sorts, making a confused screaming. Not one of them was of a kind that I knew. As for the creature I killed, I took it to be a kind of hawk, its color and beak resembling it, but it had no talons or claws more than common; its flesh was carrion and fit for nothing.

Satisfied with this discovery, I came back to my raft, and fell to work to bring my cargo to shore, which took me the rest of that day. What to do with myself at night I knew not, nor indeed where to rest. I was afraid to lie down on the ground not knowing but some wild beast might devour me, though, as I afterward found, there was really no need for those fears.

However, as well as I could, I barricaded myself round with the chests and boards that I had brought on shore, and made a kind of hut for that night's lodging. As for food, I yet saw not which way to supply myself, except that I had seen two or three creatures, like hares, run out of the wood where I shot the bird.

I now began to consider that I might yet get a great many things out of the ship which would be useful to me, and particularly some of the rigging and sails, and such other things as might come to hand, and I resolved to make another voyage on board the vessel, if possible. I knew that the first storm that blew must necessarily break her all to pieces, and I resolved to set all other things aside till I got everything out of the ship that I could get. Then I called a council, that is to say, in my thoughts, whether I should take back the raft, but this appeared impracticable, so I resolved to go as before, when the tide was down. I did so, but I stripped before I went from my hut, having nothing on but a checkered shirt and a pair of linen trousers and a pair of pumps on my feet.

I got on board the ship, as before, and prepared a

second raft, and having had experience of the first, I neither made this so unwieldy, nor loaded it so hard. Yet I brought away several things very useful to me. In the carpenter's stores I found two or three bags full of nails and spikes, a great screw jack, a dozen or two of hatchets, and, above all, that most useful thing called a grindstone. All these I secured, together with several things belonging to the gunner, particularly two or three iron crowbars, and two barrels of musket bullets, seven muskets, and another fowling piece, with some small quantity of powder more, a large bag full of small shot, and a great roll of sheet lead. However, this last was so heavy that I could not hoist it up to get it over the ship's side.

Besides these things, I took all the men's clothes that I could find and a spare fore-topsail, hammock, and some bedding. With this I loaded my second raft, and brought them all safe to shore, to my very great comfort.

I was afraid that during my absence from the land my provisions might be devoured, but when I came back, I found no sign of any visitor, except that a creature like a wild cat sat upon one of the chests. When I came toward her, she ran away a little distance, and then stood still. She sat very composed and unconcerned, and looked full in my face, as if she had a mind to be acquainted with me. I leveled my gun at her, but as she did not understand it, she was perfectly unconcerned at it, nor did she offer to stir away. At that I tossed her a bit of biscuit, though, by the way, I was not very free of it, for my store was not great. However, I spared her a bit, I say, and she went to it, smelled it, ate it, and looked for more, but I could spare no more, so she marched off.

When I had got my second cargo on shore, though I was eager to open the barrels of powder, and bring them by parcels (for they were too heavy, being large casks), I went to work to make me a little tent with the sail and some poles which I cut for that purpose. Into this tent I brought everything that I knew would spoil, either with rain or sun, and I piled all the empty chests and casks up in a circle round the tent, to fortify it from any sudden attempt, either from man or beast.

When I had done this, I blocked up the door of the tent with some boards within, and an empty chest set up on end without. Spreading a bed on the ground, and laying my two pistols just at my head, and my gun beside me, I went to bed for the first time, and slept very quietly all night, for I was very weary. The night before I had slept little, and I had worked very hard all day.

I had the biggest magazine of all kinds now that ever was laid up, I believe, for one man, but still I was not satisfied. While the ship stood upright, I thought that I ought to get everything out of her I could. Every day at low water I went on board, and brought away something or other. The third time I went, I brought away as much of the rigging as I could, as also all the small ropes and rope twine I could get, with a piece

of spare canvas, which was to mend the sails upon occasion, and also the barrel of wet gunpowder. In a
word, I brought away all the sails first and last, but I
had to cut them in pieces, and bring as much at a time
as I could, for they were no longer useful as sails, but
as mere canvas only.

But that which comforted me more still was that,
last of all, after I had made five or six such voyages
as these, and thought I had nothing more to expect
from the ship that was worth my meddling with, I
found a great hogshead of bread, and three large runlets* of rum or spirits, a box of sugar, and a barrel of
fine flour. This was surprising to me, because I had
given up expecting to find any more provisions, except what was spoiled by the water. I soon emptied
the hogshead of that bread, and wrapped it up, parcel by parcel, in pieces of the sails, which I cut out.
In a word, I got all this safe on shore also.

The next day I made another voyage. Now that I
had plundered the ship of what was portable and fit
to hand out, I began with the cables. Cutting the
great cable into pieces, such as I could move, I got two
cables and a hawser on shore, with all the ironwork I
could get. When I had cut down the spritsail-yard,
and the mizzen-yard, and everything I could to make a
large raft, I loaded it with all those heavy goods and
came away. But my good luck began now to leave
me, for this raft was so unwieldy and so overloaded,
that after I had entered the little cove, where I had

---

* Runlet: An obsolete word for "rundlet," a wine barrel.

landed the rest of my goods, I could not guide it so handily as I did the other, and it upset and threw me and all my cargo into the water. As for myself it was no great harm, for I was near the shore, but a great part of my cargo was lost, especially the iron, which I had thought would be of great use to me. However, when the tide was out, I got most of the pieces of cable ashore, and some of the iron, though with infinite labor, for I had to dip for it into the water—a work which fatigued me very much. After this, I went every day on board and brought away what I could get.

I had been now thirteen days on shore, and had been eleven times on board the ship, in which time I had brought away all that one pair of hands could be well supposed capable to bring, though I verily believe, had the calm weather held, I should have brought away the whole ship, piece by piece. But as I prepared the twelfth time to go on board, I found that the wind had begun to rise. However, at low water I went on board, and though I thought I had rummaged the cabin so effectually that nothing more could be found, yet I discovered a locker with drawers in it, in one of which I found two or three razors and one pair of large scissors, with some ten or a dozen good knives and forks. In another I found about thirty-six pounds value in money, some European coin, some Brazil, some pieces of eight, some gold, some silver.

Wrapping all that I had found in a piece of canvas,

I began to think of making another raft, but while I was preparing this, I found the sky overcast, and the wind rising, and in a quarter of an hour it blew a fresh gale from the shore. It presently occurred to me that it was in vain to pretend to make a raft with the wind offshore, and that it was my business to be gone before the tide of flood began. Otherwise I might not be able to reach the shore at all. Accordingly, I let myself down into the water, and swam across the channel which lay between the ship and the sands, and even that with difficulty enough, partly because of the weight of things I had about me, and partly because of the roughness of the water. The wind rose very hastily, and before it was quite high water it blew a storm.

But I was home in my little tent, where I lay very secure with all my wealth about me. It blew very hard all that night, and in the morning no more ship was to be seen.

Building My Home ～

My thoughts were now wholly employed with securing myself against either savages, if any should appear, or wild beasts, if any were in the island. I had many thoughts of the method how to do this, and what kind of dwelling to make. I considered whether I should make a cave in the earth, or a tent upon the earth, and, finally I decided upon both.

I soon found that the place I was in was not suitable for my home, partly because it was low, marshy ground near the sea, and more particularly because there was no fresh water near it. Accordingly I resolved to find a more healthy and more convenient spot of ground.

I considered several things in choosing my location: health and fresh water, I just now mentioned; shelter from the heat of the sun; security from ravenous creatures, whether man or beast; a view of the sea, so that if God sent any ship in sight, I might not lose any advantage for my deliverance, of which I was not willing to banish all hope yet.

In search of a place proper for this, I found a little plain on the side of a rising hill. The front toward this little plain was as steep as a house side, so that nothing could come down upon me from the top. On the side of this rock there was a hollow place, worn a little way in, like the entrance or door of a cave, but there was not really any cave or way into the rock at all.

On the flat of the green, just before this hollow place, I resolved to pitch my tent. This plain was not above a hundred yards broad, and about twice as long, and lay like a green before my door. At the end it descended irregularly into the low grounds by the seaside. It was on the NNW. side of the hill, so that I was sheltered from the heat every day, till it came to a W. and by S. sun, or thereabouts, which in those countries is near the setting.

Before I set up my tent, I drew a half circle before the hollow place, which took in about ten yards in its semidiameter, from the rock, and twenty yards in its diameter, from its beginning and ending.

In this half circle I pitched two rows of strong stakes, driving them into the ground till they stood very firm, like piles, the biggest end being out of the ground about five feet and a half, and sharpened on the top. The two rows did not stand more than six inches from one another.

Then I took the pieces of cable which I had cut in the ship, and laid them in rows one upon another, within the circle between these two rows of stakes, up to the top. I placed other stakes in the inside, leaning against them, about two foot and a half high, like a spur to a post. This fence was so strong that neither man nor beast could get into it or over it. This cost me a great deal of time and labor, especially to cut the piles in the woods, bring them to the place, and drive them into the earth.

The entrance into this place I made to be not by a door, but by a short ladder to go over the top. When I was in, I lifted the ladder over after me, and so I was completely fenced in and fortified, as I thought, from all the world. Consquently I slept secure in the night, which otherwise I could not have done. As it appeared afterward, however, there was no need of all this caution from the enemies that I feared.

Into this fence or fortress, with infinite labor, I carried all my riches, all my provisions, ammunition, and stores, of which you have the account above. To protect me from the rains, which in one part of the year are very violent there, I made a large, double tent, one smaller tent within, and one larger tent above it. I covered the uppermost with a large tarpaulin which I had saved among the sails.

I no longer slept in the bed which I had brought on shore, but in a hammock, which was indeed a very good one, and had belonged to the mate of the ship.

Into my tent I brought all my provisions, and everything that would spoil by the wet. When I had brought my goods I closed up the entrance, which till

now I had left open, and after that passed and re-passed, as I said, by a short ladder.

When I had done this, I began to work my way into the rock. I brought all the earth and stones that I dug down out through my tent, and laid them up within my fence in the nature of a terrace so that it raised the ground about a foot and a half. Thus I made a cave just behind my tent, which served me as a cellar to my house.

It cost me much labor and many days, before all these things were brought to perfection, and there-

fore I must go back to some other things which took
up some of my thoughts. At the same time it happened, after I had laid my scheme for setting up my
tent and making the cave, that a storm of rain fell from
a thick, dark cloud, there was a sudden flash of lightning, and after that a great clap of thunder. I was not
so much surprised by the lightning, as I was terrified
by a thought which darted into my mind as swift as
the lightning itself. My powder! My very heart sank
within me, when I thought that at one blast all my
powder might be destroyed, on which, not my defense only, but the providing food, as I thought, entirely depended. I was not nearly so anxious about
my own danger, although, had the powder taken fire,
I should never have know what had hurt me.

Such impression did this make upon me, that after
the storm was over I laid aside all my works, my building and fortifying, and applied myself to making bags
and boxes to separate the powder. I put but little in
each package and then hid the box, or bag, in the rocks
as far from the others as I could. I did this in the hope
that even if one part of my powder was struck, the rest
might be saved. I finished this work in about a fortnight, and I think my powder, which in all was about
two hundred and forty pounds, was divided in not less
than a hundred parcels. As to the barrel that had
been wet, I did not expect any danger from that, so
I placed it in my new cave, which, in my fancy, I
called my kitchen. The rest I hid up and down in

holes among the rocks, so that no wet might come to it, marking very carefully where I laid it.

In the interval of time while I was doing this, I went out once at least every day with my gun, as well to divert myself as to see if I could kill anything fit for food, and, as near as I could, to acquaint myself with what the island produced. The first time I went out I presently discovered that there were goats in the island, which was a great satisfaction to me, but then it was attended with this misfortune, that they were so shy, so subtle, and so swift of foot, that it was the most difficult thing in the world to come at them. But I was not discouraged at this, not doubting that I might now and then shoot one, as it soon happened. After I had found their haunts, I laid wait in this manner for them. I observed that if they saw me in the valleys, though they were upon the rocks, they would run away as in a terrible fright, but if they were feeding in the valleys, and I was upon the rocks, they took no notice of me. From this I concluded that by the position of their eyes, their sight was so directed downward, that they did not readily see objects that were above them, so afterward I took this method. I always climbed the rocks first, to get above them, and then I had frequently a fair mark. The first shot I made among these creatures I killed a she-goat, which had a little kid by her. This grieved me greatly, but when the old one fell, the kid stood stockstill by her till I came and took her up. Not only so, but when

I carried the old one with me upon my shoulders, the kid followed me quite to my enclosure. Upon this I laid down the dam, and took the kid in my arms and carried it over my pale, in the hope of taming it, but it would not eat, so I was forced to kill it and eat it myself. These two supplied me with flesh a great while, for I ate sparingly, and saved my provisions (my bread especially) as much as I possibly could.

Now that I had fixed my habitation, I found it absolutely necessary to provide a place to make a fire in, and fuel to burn. What I did for that, as also how I enlarged my cave, and what conveniences I made, I shall give a full account of in its place, but I must first give some little account of myself, and of my thoughts about living, which it may well be supposed were not a few.

My outlook was dismal, for as I was not cast away upon that island without being driven, as is said, by a violent storm quite out of the course of our intended voyage, and a great way, some hundreds of leagues, out of the ordinary course of the trade of mankind, I had great reason to consider it as a determination of heaven that in this desolate place and in this desolate manner, I should end my life.

And now being about to enter into the melancholy story of a scene of silent life, such, perhaps, as was never heard of in the world before, I shall take it from its beginning, and continue it in its order. It was, by my account, the 30th of September, when, in the manner as above said, I first set foot upon this horrid

island. The sun being, to us, in its autumnal equinox, was almost directly over my head. I reckoned myself, by observation, to be in the latitude of 9 degrees and 22 minutes north of the line.

After I had been there about ten or twelve days, it came into my thoughts that I should lose my reckoning of time for want of books and pen and ink, and should even confuse the Sabbath days with the working days. To prevent this, I cut with my knife upon a large post in capital letters, I CAME ON SHORE HERE ON THE 30TH OF SEPT., 1659. Making it into a great cross, I set it up on the shore where I first landed. Upon the sides of this square post I cut every day a notch with my knife, and every seventh notch was as long

again as the rest, and every first day of the month
as long again as that long one; and thus I kept my cal-
endar, or weekly, monthly, and yearly reckoning of
time.

In the next place we are to observe that, among the
many things which I brought out of the ship in the
several voyages which I made to it, I got several things
of less value, but not all less useful to me, which I
omitted setting down before: in particular, pens, ink,
and paper; several parcels in the captain's, mate's,
gunner's, and carpenter's keeping; three or four com-
passes, some mathematical instruments, dials, perspective glasses, charts, and books of navigation. All these
I huddled together, whether I might want them or not.
Also I found three very good Bibles which came to
me in my cargo from England, and which I had
packed up among my things. There were some Portuguese books, also, and among them two or three
popish prayer books, and several other books, all of
which I carefully secured. And I must not forget that
we had in the ship a dog and two cats, of whose history I may have occasion to say something in its place.
I carried both the cats with me and the dog jumped
out of the ship himself, and swam on shore to me the
day after I went on shore with my first cargo. He
was a trusty servant to me for many years. I wanted
nothing that he could bring me, or any company that
he could make up to me; I only wanted to have him
talk to me, but that he could not do. As I observed
before, I found pen, ink, and paper, and I husbanded

them to the utmost; I shall show that, while my ink lasted, I kept things very exact, but after that was gone I could not, for I could not make any ink, by any means that I could devise.

This put me in mind that I wanted many things, notwithstanding all that I had gathered together. Of these ink was one, as were a spade, a pickax, and a shovel, to dig or remove the earth; needles, pins, and thread. As for linen, I soon learned to do without that without much difficulty.

This want of tools made every work I did go on heavily, and it was nearly a whole year before I had entirely finished my little pale and my dwelling. The piles or stakes, which were as heavy as I could well lift, took a long time to cut and prepare in the woods, and more by far to bring home, so that I spent sometimes two days in cutting and bringing home one of those posts, and a third day in driving it into the ground. For this purpose I got a heavy piece of wood at first, but at last I thought of using one of the iron crowbars. Even with this, driving those posts or piles was very tiresome and tedious work.

But I had no need to be concerned at the tediousness of anything I had to do, seeing I had time enough to do it in, nor had I any other employment if that had been over, at least that I could foresee, except ranging the island to seek for food, which I did more or less every day.

I have already described my habitation, which was a tent under the side of a rock, surrounded with a

strong pale of posts and cables, but I might now rather
call it a wall, for I raised a kind of wall up against it
of turf, about two feet thick on the outside. After
some time, I think it was a year and a half, I raised
rafters from it, leaning to the rock, and thatched or
covered it with boughs of trees and such things as I
could get to keep out the rain, which I found at some
times of the year very violent.

I have already observed how I brought all my goods
into this pale, and into the cave which I had made
behind me. At first this was a confused heap of goods,
which, as they lay in no order, took up all my place so
that I had no room to turn myself. Accordingly, I
set to work to enlarge my cave and work farther into
the earth, for it was a loose, sandy rock, which yielded
easily to the labor I bestowed on it. When I found
I was pretty safe as to beasts of prey, I worked side-
ways to the right hand into the rock, and then turning
to the right again, worked quite out, and made a door
to come out, on the outside of my pale or fortification.

This gave me not only a way of going in and out,
as it were a back way to my tent and to my storehouse,
but it gave me also room to stow my goods.

And now I began to apply myself to make such
necessary things as I found I most wanted, particularly
a chair and a table, for without these I was not able to
enjoy the few comforts I had. I could not write or
eat, or do several things, with much pleasure without
a table.

So I went to work, and here I must needs observe that, as reason is the substance and original of the mathematics, so by stating and squaring everything by reason, and by making the most rational judgment of things, every man may be in time master of every mechanic art. I had never handled a tool in my life, and yet in time by labor, application, and contrivance, I found at last that I wanted nothing that I could not have made, if I had had the right tools. However, I made an abundance of things, even without proper tools, and some with no more tools than an adz and a hatchet (which, perhaps, were never made that way before, and that with infinite labor). If I wanted a board, I had no other way but to cut down a tree, hew it flat on either side with my ax, till I had made it as thin as a plank, and then rub it smooth with my adz. It is true that by this method I could make but one board out of a whole tree, but I had no remedy for this, any more than I had for the prodigious deal of time and labor which it took me up to make a plank or board. My time or labor was worth little, however, and so it was as well employed one way as another.

However, I first made a table and a chair, as I observed above, and this I did out of the short pieces of boards which I brought on my raft from the ship. When I had hewed out some boards, I made large shelves, of the breadth of a foot and a half, one over another, all along one side of my cave, where I laid

all my tools, nails, and ironwork. I knocked pieces
into the wall of the rock to hold my guns and all things
that would hang up.

As a result, my cave looked like a general magazine
of all necessary things. I had everything so ready to
my hand that it was a great pleasure to me to see all my
goods in such order, and especially to find my stock of
all necessaries so great.

And now it was that I began to keep a journal of
every day's employment. Before this I was in too
much hurry, and not only hurry as to labor, but in too
much distress of mind, and my journal would have
been full of many dull things.

I shall here give you the copy (though in it will be
told many particulars over again) as long as it lasted.
As I have said, when I had no more ink, I was forced
to give up.

THE JOURNAL

September 30, 1659. I, poor, miserable Robinson
Crusoe, being shipwrecked during a dreadful storm
in the offing, came on shore on this dismal, unfortunate island, which I called the Island of Despair. All
the rest of the ship's company were drowned, and I
myself was almost dead.

All the rest of that day I spent in pitying myself
because of the dismal circumstances I was brought to.
I had neither food, house, clothes, weapon, nor place
to fly to, and in despair of any relief, I saw nothing
but death before me, either that I should be devoured
by wild beasts, murdered by savages, or starved to

death for want of food. At the approach of night I slept in a tree, for fear of wild creatures, but I slept soundly though it rained all night.

October 1. In the morning I saw, to my great surprise, that the ship had floated with the high tide, and was driven on shore again much nearer the island. This was some comfort, on one hand, for seeing her stand upright and not broken to pieces, I hoped, if the wind abated, to get on board and get some food or necessaries out of her for my relief. On the other hand, it renewed my grief at the loss of my comrades, for I imagined if we had all stayed on board we might have saved the ship. At least they would not all have been drowned, as they were, and, had the men been saved, we might perhaps have built us a boat out of the ruins of the ship, to have carried us to some other part of the world. I spent a great part of this day in perplexing myself on these things; but at length, seeing the ship almost dry, I went upon the sand as near as I could, and then swam on board. This day also it continued raining, though with no wind at all.

From the 1st of October to the 24th. All these days were entirely spent in making several voyages to get all I could out of the ship, which I brought on shore, every tide of flood, upon rafts. There was much rain also in these days, though with some intervals of fair weather, but it seems that this was the rainy season.

October 20. I upset my raft, and all the goods I had upon it; but being in shoal water, and the things being chiefly heavy, I recovered many of them when the tide was out.

October 25. It rained all night and all day, with some gusts of wind, during which time the ship broke in pieces, the wind blowing a little harder than before, and was no more to be seen, except the wreck of her, and that only at low water. I spent this day in covering and securing the goods which I had saved, that the rain might not spoil them.

October 26. I walked about the shore almost all day, to find out a place to fix my habitation, greatly concerned to secure myself from any attack in the night, either from wild beasts or men. Toward night I fixed upon a proper place under a rock, and marked out a semicircle for my encampment, which I resolved to strengthen with a work, wall, or fortification made of double piles, lined within with cables, and without with turf.

From the 26th to the 30th, I worked very hard in carrying all my goods to my new habitation, though some part of the time it rained exceedingly hard.

The 31st, in the morning, I went out into the island with my gun to look for some food and discover the country, when I killed a she-goat, and her kid followed me home. The kid I afterward killed, also, because it would not feed.

November 1. I set up my tent under a rock, and lay there for the first night, making it as large as I could with stakes driven in to swing my hammock upon.

November 2. I set up all my chests and boards and the pieces of timber which made my rafts, and with them formed a fence round me, a little within the place I had marked out for my fortifications.

November 3. I went out with my gun and killed two fowls like ducks, which were very good food. In the afternoon I went to work to make a table.

November 4. This morning I began to order my times of work, of going out with my gun, time of sleep, and time of diversion. Every morning I walked out with my gun for two or three hours, if it did not rain, then employed myself to work till about eleven o'clock, then ate what I had to live on. From twelve to two I lay down to sleep, the weather being excessive hot, and in the evening I worked again. The working part of this day, and of the next, were wholly employed in making my table, for I was yet but a very poor workman.

November 5. This day I went abroad with my gun and my dog, and killed a wild cat. Her skin was pretty soft, but her flesh was good for nothing. Every creature I killed I took off the skins and preserved them. Coming back by the seashore I saw many sorts of seafowls, which I did not know. I was surprised and almost frightened when I saw two or three seals. While I was gazing, not well knowing what they were, they slipped into the sea, and escaped me for that time.

November 6. After my morning walk I went to work with my table again, and finished it, though not to my liking; nor was it long before I learned to mend it.

November 7. Now it began to be settled fair weather. The 7th, 8th, 9th, 10th, and a part of the 12th (for the 11th was Sunday), I took wholly to make a chair. With much ado I brought it to a tolerable shape, but never to please me, and even in the making I pulled it in pieces several times. *Note.—* I soon neglected my keeping Sundays, for omitting my mark for them on my post, I forgot which was which.

November 13. This day it rained, which refreshed me exceedingly, and cooled the earth; but it was accompanied with terrible thunder and lightning, which frightened me dreadfully for fear of my powder. As soon as it was over I resolved to separate my stock of powder into as many little parcels as possible, that it might not be in danger.

November 14, 15, 16. These three days I spent in making little square chests or boxes, which might hold about a pound, or two pounds at most, of powder. Putting the powder in them, I stowed it in places as secure and remote from one another as possible. On one of these three days I killed a large bird that was good to eat, but I know not what to call it.

November 17. This day I began to dig behind my tent into the rock, to make room for my farther conveniency. *Note.*—Three things I wanted exceeding for this work, namely, a pickax, a shovel, and a wheel-

barrow or basket, so I stopped my work and began
to consider how to supply that want and make me
some tools. As for a pickax, I made use of the iron
crowbars, which were proper enough, though heavy;
but the next thing was a shovel or spade. This was
so absolutely necessary, that indeed I could do nothing effectually without it, but what kind of one to
make I knew not.

November 18. The next day, in searching the
woods, I found a tree of that wood, or like it, which
in the Brazils they call the Iron Tree, for its exceeding hardness. Of this, with great labor and almost
spoiling my ax, I cut a piece and brought it home with
difficulty enough, for it was exceedingly heavy.

The excessive hardness of the wood kept me a long
while upon this tool, but I worked it effectually little
by little into the form of a shovel or spade. The handle was shaped exactly like ours in England, only that
the broad part had no iron shod upon it at bottom.
It would not last me long, but it served well enough
for the uses which I put it to. Never was a shovel,
I believe, made after that fashion, or so long amaking.

I was not yet satisfied, for I wanted a basket or a
wheelbarrow. A basket I could not make by any
means, for I had no such things as twigs that would
bend to make wickerware, or at least I had not found
any. As for a wheelbarrow, I fancied that I could
make all but the wheel, but that I had no notion of,
neither did I know how to go about it. Besides, I had
no possible way to make the iron gudgeons for the

spindle or axis of the wheel to run in, so I gave it up. For carrying away the earth which I dug out of the cave, I made a thing like a hod, which the laborers carry mortar in.

This was not so difficult to me as making the shovel, and yet this and the shovel and the attempt which I made in vain to make a wheelbarrow, took me no less than four days, always excepting my morning walk with my gun. I seldom failed to take that and very seldom failed to bring home something to eat.

November 23. My other work had stood still because of my making these tools, and when they were finished I went on. Working every day, as my strength and time allowed, I spent eighteen days entirely in widening and deepening my cave, that it might hold my goods comfortably.

Note.—During all this time I worked to make this room or cave spacious enough to accommodate me as a warehouse or magazine, a kitchen, a dining room, and a cellar. As for my lodging, I kept to the tent, except that sometimes in the wet season of the year, it rained so hard that I could not keep myself dry, which caused me afterward to cover all my place within my pale with long poles in the form of rafters, leaning against the rock, and load them with flags and large leaves of trees like a thatch.

December 10. I began now to think my cave or vault finished, when suddenly (it seems that I had made it too large) a great quantity of earth fell down from the top and one side. I was frightened and not without reason, for if I had been under it, I should never have wanted a gravedigger. After this disaster I had a great deal of work to do over again, for I had the loose earth to carry out, and, which was of more importance, I had the ceiling to prop up, so that I might be sure no more would come down.

December 11. Today I went to work at it, accordingly, and got two shores or posts pitched upright to the top, with two pieces of boards across over each post. This I finished the next day, and setting more posts up with boards, in about a week more I had the roof secured, and the posts, standing in rows, served me for partitions to divide off my house.

December 17. From this day to the twentieth I placed shelves, and knocked up nails on the posts to hang everything up that could be hung up, and now I began to be in some order within doors.

December 20. Now I carried everything into the cave, and began to furnish my house, and set up some pieces of boards, like a dresser, to put my food upon. Also, I made another table.

December 24. Much rain all night and all day; no stirring out.

December 25. Rain all day.

December 26. No rain, the earth much cooler than before, and pleasanter.

December 27. Killed a young goat, and lamed another, so that I caught it, and led it home on a string. When I had it home, I bound and splintered up its leg, which was broken. *Note.*—I took such care of it that it lived, and the leg grew well and as strong as ever, but I had nursed it so long it grew tame, and fed upon the little green at my door, and would not go away. This was the first time that I entertained a thought of breeding some tame creatures, that I might have food when my powder and shot were all spent.

December 28, 29, 30. Great heat and no breeze, so that there was no stirring abroad, except in the evening for food. This time I spent in putting all my things in order within doors.

January 1. Very hot still, but I went abroad early and late with my gun, and lay still in the middle of the day. This evening, I went farther into the valley, which lay toward the center of the island, and found there plenty of goats, though they were exceedingly shy and hard to come at. However, I resolved to bring my dog to try to hunt them down.

January 2. Accordingly, the next day, I went out with my dog, and set him upon the goats, but I was mistaken, for they all faced about upon the dog, and he knew his danger too well, for he would not go near them.

January 3. I began my fence or wall, and since I was still afraid of being attacked by somebody, I resolved to make it very thick and strong.

Note.—This wall, being described before, I purposely omit what was said in the Journal. It is sufficient to observe that I was no less time than from the 3d of January to the 14th of April, working, finishing, and perfecting this wall, though it was no more than about twenty-four yards in length, being a half circle from one place in the rock to another place about eight yards from it. The door of the cave was in the center behind it.

All this time I worked very hard, the rains hindering me many days, nay, sometimes weeks together, but I thought I should never be perfectly secure until this wall was finished. It is scarcely credible what inexpressible labor everything was done with, especially the bringing piles out of the woods, and driving them into the ground, for I made them much bigger than I needed to have done.

When this wall was finished and the outside double fence with a turf wall raised up close to it, I persuaded myself that if any people were to come on shore there, they would not see anything like a dwelling. It was very well I did so, as may be observed hereafter upon a very remarkable occasion.

During this time I made my rounds in the woods for game every day, when the rain permitted me, and made frequent discoveries in these walks of something or other to my advantage. One time I found a kind of wild pigeon, who built not as wood pigeons, in a tree, but rather as house pigeons, in the holes of the rocks. Taking some young ones, I endeavored to tame them and did so, but when they grew older they flew away. This may have been because I did not feed them, for I had nothing to give them. However, I frequently found their nests and got their young ones, which were very good meat.

And now, in the managing my household affairs, I found myself wanting in many things, which I thought at first it was impossible for me to make, as indeed, in some cases, it was. For instance, I could never make a cask to be hooped. I had a small runlet or two, as I observed before, but I could never make one by copying them, though I spent many weeks about it. I could neither put in the heads, or joint the staves so true to one another as to make them hold water, so I gave that up, also.

In the next place, I was at a great loss for a candle. As soon as it was dark, which was generally by seven o'clock, I was obliged to go to bed. I remembered the lump of beeswax with which I made candles in my African adventure, but I had none of that now. The only remedy I had was that when I had killed a goat I saved the tallow, and with a little dish made of clay, which I baked in the sun, to which I added a wick of some oakum, I made a lamp. This gave me light, though not a clear, steady light like a candle. In the middle of all my labors it happened that as I rummaged among my things, I found a little bag, which, as I hinted before, had been filled with grain for the feeding of poultry. What little grain had remained in the bag was devoured by the rats, and I saw nothing in the bag but husks and dust. I wanted the bag for some other use, so I shook the husks of grain out of it on one side of my fortification under the rock.

It was a little before the great rains, just now mentioned, that I threw this stuff away, taking no notice of anything, and not so much as remembering that I had thrown anything there. About a month after, or thereabouts, I saw some few stalks of something green shooting out of the ground, which I fancied might be some plant I had not seen. I was surprised and perfectly astonished when, after a little longer time, I saw about ten or twelve ears come out, which were perfect green barley of the same kind as our English barley.

It is impossible to express the astonishment and confusion of my thoughts on this occasion. I had hitherto acted upon no religious foundation at all; indeed, I had very few notions of religion in my head, and had not entertained any sense of anything that had befallen me, otherwise, than as a chance, or, as we lightly say, what pleases God. I had not so much as inquired into the end of Providence in these things, or His order in governing events in the world, but after I saw barley grow there, in a climate which I knew was not proper for grain, and especially when I did not know how it came there, it startled me strangely. I began to think that God had miraculously caused this grain to grow without any help of seed sown, and that it was so directed purely for my sustenance on that wild, miserable place.

This touched my heart a little, and brought tears

out of my eyes, and I began to think myself fortunate that such a prodigy of nature should happen upon my account. This was the more strange to me, because I saw near it, all along by the side of the rock, some other straggling stalks, which proved to be stalks of rice, and which I knew, because I had seen it grow in Africa, when I was ashore there.

I not only thought these the pure productions of Providence for my support, but not doubting but that there was more in the place, I went all over that part of the island, where I had been before, peeping in every corner and under every rock to see more of it, but I could not find any. At last it occurred to my thought that I had shaken a bag of grain out in that place, and then the wonder began to cease. And I must confess, my religious thankfulness to God's providence began to abate too, upon discovering that all this was nothing but what was common, though I ought to have been as thankful for so strange and unforeseen a providence as if it had been miraculous. It was really the work of Providence, that ten or twelve grains had remained unspoiled, when the rats had destroyed all the rest. It was the work of Providence, too, that I had thrown it out in that particular place, where, since it was in the shade of a high rock, it sprang up immediately. If I had thrown it anywhere else at that time it would have been burned up and destroyed.

I carefully saved the grain, you may be sure, in its season, which was about the end of June, and resolved to sow it all again, hoping in time to have some quantity sufficient to supply me with bread. It was not till the fourth year, however, that I could allow myself the least particle of this grain to eat, and even then but sparingly, as I shall tell afterward in its order. I lost all that I sowed the first season by not observing the proper time, for I sowed it just before the dry season, so that it never came up at all.

Besides this barley, there were, as I said, twenty or thirty stalks of rice, which I preserved with the same care. Their use was the same, to make me bread, or rather food, for I found ways to cook it without baking, though I did that also after some time. But to return to my Journal.

I worked extremely hard these three or four months to get my wall done. The 14th of April I closed it up, contriving to go into it not by a door, but over the wall by a ladder, that there might be no sign on the outside of my dwelling.

April 16. I finished the ladder, so I went up with the ladder to the top, and then pulled it up after me, and let it down on the inside. This was a complete enclosure for me. Within I had room enough, and nothing could come at me from without, unless it could first mount my wall.

After the Earthquake

THE very next day after this wall was finished, I almost had all my labor overthrown at once, and myself killed. As I was busy inside the wall, behind my tent, just in the entrance into my cave, I was terribly frighted with a most dreadful surprising thing indeed. Suddenly the earth came crumbling down from the roof of my cave, and from the edge of the hill, over my head, and two of the posts I had set up in the cave cracked in a frightful manner. I was heartily scared, but thought nothing of what was really the cause, only thinking that the top of my cave was falling in, as some of it had done before. For fear I should be buried in it, I ran forward to my ladder, and not thinking myself safe there either, I got over my wall for fear of the pieces of the hill which I expected might roll down upon me. I was no sooner stepped down upon the ground than I plainly saw that it was a terrible earthquake, for the ground I stood on shook three times at about eight minutes' distance, with three such shocks as would have overturned the strongest building that could be supposed to have stood on the earth. A great piece of the top of a rock, which stood about half a mile from me next the sea, fell down with a terrible noise such as I never had heard before in all my life. I perceived also that the very sea was put into violent motion by it, and I believe that the shocks were stronger under the water than on the island.

I was so amazed with the thing itself, having never felt the like, or talked with anyone that had, that I was like one dead or stupefied. The motion of the earth made my stomach sick, like one that was tossed at sea. But the noise of the falling of the rock awakened me, as it were, and rousing me from the stupefied condition I was in, filled me with horror, and I thought of nothing then but the hill falling upon my tent, and all my household goods, and burying all at once. This sank my very soul within me a second time.

After the third shock was over, and I felt no more for some time, I began to take courage, and yet I had not heart enough to get over my wall again, for fear of being buried alive. I sat still upon the ground, greatly cast down and disconsolate, not knowing what to do. All this while I had not the least serious religious thought, nothing but the common, "Lord, have mercy upon me," and when it was over, that went away, too.

While I sat thus, I saw that the sky was growing overcast and cloudy, as if it would rain. Soon after that the wind rose little by little, so that in less than half an hour it blew a most dreadful hurricane. The sea was suddenly covered over with foam and froth, the shore washed with huge waves, the trees torn up by the roots. In short, it was a terrible storm. This lasted about three hours, and then began to abate, and in two hours more it was stark calm, and began to rain very hard.

All this while I sat upon the ground, very much terrified and dejected. Suddenly it came into my thoughts that these winds and the rain being the consequences of the earthquake, the earthquake itself was spent and over, and I might venture into my cave again. With this thought my spirits began to revive, and the rain also helping to persuade me, I went in and sat down in my tent, but the rain was so violent, that my tent was ready to be beaten down with it. I was forced to go into my cave, though I was very uneasy, for fear it should fall on my head.

This violent rain forced me to a new work, to cut a hole through my new fortification like a sink to let water go out, which otherwise would have filled my cave. After I had been in my cave some time, and had found that no more shocks of the earthquake followed, I began to be more composed. And now, to support my spirits, which indeed wanted it very much, I went to my little store, and took a small sup of rum, which however I did then, and always, very sparingly, knowing that I could have no more when that was gone.

It continued raining all that night and a great part of the next day, so that I could not stir abroad, but my mind was more composed and I began to think what I had best do. I concluded that if the island was subject to these earthquakes, there would be no living for me in a cave, but I must consider building some little hut in an open place. I could surround it with a wall as I had done here, and so make myself secure from wild beasts or men. I was convinced that if I stayed where I was, I should certainly, one time or other, be buried alive.

With these thoughts I resolved to remove my tent from the place where it stood. It was just under the hanging precipice of the hill, which, if it should be shaken again, would certainly fall upon my tent. I spent the next two days, the 19th and 20th of April, in planning where and how to remove my habitation.

I was so afraid of being swallowed alive that I never slept in quiet, yet my terror at lying out in the open without a fence was almost equal to it. When I looked about and saw how everything was put in order, how pleasantly concealed I was, and how safe from danger, it made me very loath to remove.

In the meantime, it occurred to me that it would require a great deal of time for me to do this, and that I must be contented to run the risk where I was, till I had formed a camp for myself, and had secured it so that I could move to it. With this resolution I composed myself for a time, and resolved that I would go to work with all speed to build a wall with piles and cables, in a circle as before, and set my tent up in it when it was finished, but that I would venture to stay where I was till it was finished and fit to move to. This was the 21st.

April 22. The next morning I began to consider means to put this resolve into execution, but I was at a great loss about my tools. I had three large axes and an abundance of hatchets (for we carried the hatchets for traffic with the Indians), but with much chopping and cutting knotty, hard wood, they were all full of notches and dull, and though I had a grindstone, I could not turn it and grind my tools, too. This cost me as much thought as a statesman would have bestowed upon a grand point of politics, or a judge upon the life and death of a man. At length I contrived a wheel with a string, to turn it with my foot, that I might have both my hands at liberty. I had never seen any such thing in England, or at least not to take notice how it was done, though since I have observed it is very common there. This machine cost me a full week's work to bring it to perfection.

April 28, 29. These two whole days I took up in grinding my tools, my machine for turning my grindstone performing very well.

April 30. Having perceived that my bread had been low a great while, now I took a survey of it, and reduced myself to one biscuit cake a day, which made my heart very heavy.

May 1. In the morning, when I looked toward

the seaside, the tide being low, I saw something bigger than ordinary lying on the shore. It looked like a cask. When I came to it, I found a small barrel and two or three pieces of the wreck of the ship, which had been driven on shore by the recent hurricane. When I looked toward the wreck itself, I thought it seemed to lie higher out of the water than it used to do. I examined the barrel which was driven on shore, and soon found that it was a barrel of gunpowder, but it had taken water, and the powder was caked as hard as a stone. However, I rolled it farther on shore for the present, and went on upon the sands as near as I could to the wreck of the ship, to look for more.

When I came down to the ship, I found it strangely changed. The forecastle, which before lay buried in sand, was heaved up at least six feet. The stern, which had been broken to pieces and parted from the rest by the force of the sea soon after I had stopped rummaging her, was tossed up, as it were, and cast on one side. The sand was thrown so high on that side next her stern, that whereas there was a great place of water before, so that I could not come within a quarter of a mile of the wreck without swimming, I could now walk quite up to her when the tide was out. I was surprised with this at first, but soon concluded that it must have been done by the earthquake. By this violence the ship was more broken open than formerly, and many things came daily on shore, which the sea had loosened, and which the winds and the water rolled by degrees to the land.

This wholly diverted my thoughts from the plan of
moving my dwelling. I busied myself mightily, that
day especially, in searching whether I could make
any way into the ship, but I found that nothing was
to be expected of that kind, because all the inside of
the ship was choked up with sand. However, as I
had learned not to despair of anything, I resolved to
pull everything to pieces that I could of the ship,
concluding that everything I could get from her
would be of some use or other to me.

May 3. I began with my saw, and cut a piece of
a beam through, which I thought held some of the
upper part or quarter-deck together. When I had
cut it through, I cleared away the sand as well as I
could from the side which lay highest, but the tide
came in, and I was obliged to give up for that time.

May 4. I went fishing, but caught not one fish
that I dared eat. I was weary of my sport and was
just going to stop, when I caught a young dolphin.
I had made a long line of some rope yarn, but I had
no hooks, yet I frequently caught fish enough, as
much as I cared to eat. I dried them in the sun, and
ate them dry.

May 5. Worked on the wreck, cut another beam
asunder, and brought three great fir planks off from
the decks, which I tied together, and floated to shore
when the tide was in.

May 6. Worked on the wreck, got several iron
bolts out of her, and other pieces of ironwork;

worked very hard, and came home very tired, and had thoughts of giving it up.

May 7. Went to the wreck again, intending not to work, but found that the weight of the wreck had broken itself down. The beams were cut, so that several pieces of the ship seemed to lie loose. The inside of the hold lay so open that I could see into it, but it was almost full of water and sand.

May 8. Went to the wreck, and carried an iron crowbar to wrench up the deck, which now lay quite clear of the water or sand. I wrenched open two planks, and brought them to shore, also with the tide.

May 9. Went to the wreck, and with the crowbar made way into the body of the wreck, and felt several casks, and loosened them with the crowbar, but could not break them up. I felt also the roll of English lead, and could stir it, but it was too heavy to remove.

May 10, 11, 12, 13, 14. Went every day to the wreck, and got a great many pieces of timber and boards, or plank, and two or three hundredweight of iron.

May 15. I carried two hatchets, to try to cut a piece off the roll of lead, by placing the edge of one hatchet, and driving it with the other, but since it lay about a foot and a half in the water, I could not make any blow to drive the hatchet.

May 16. It had blown hard in the night, and the wreck appeared more broken by the force of the water, but I stayed so long in the woods to get pigeons for food that the tide prevented my going to the wreck that day.

May 17. I saw some pieces of the wreck blown on shore, at a great distance, nearly two miles away. I resolved to see what they were, and found that it was a piece of the lead, but too heavy for me to bring away.

May 24. Every day to this day I worked on the wreck, and with hard labor I loosened some things so much with the crowbar, that the first blowing tide several casks floated out, and two of the seamen's chests. The wind was blowing from the shore, however, and nothing came to land that day but pieces of timber and a hogshead, which had some Brazil pork in it, but the salt water and the sand had spoiled it.

I continued this work every day to the 15th of June, except the time necessary to get food, which I always appointed, during this part of my employment, to be when the tide was up, that I might be ready when it ebbed out. By this time I had gotten timber and plank and ironwork enough to have built a good boat, if I had known how. Also, I secured at several times, and in several pieces, almost a hundredweight of the sheet lead.

June 16. Going down to the seaside, I found a large tortoise or turtle. This was the first I had seen, which it seems was only my misfortune, not any defect of the place, or scarcity, for had I happened to be on the other side of the island I might have had hundreds of them every day. I found them afterward and perhaps paid dearly enough for them.

June 17. I spent the day cooking the turtle. I found in her threescore eggs. Her flesh was to me at that time the most savory and pleasant that ever I tasted in my life, for I had had no flesh but that of goats and fowls since I had landed in this horrid place.

June 18. Rained all day, and I stayed within. I thought at this time that the rain felt cold, and I was something chilly, which I knew was not usual in that latitude.

June 19. Very ill, and shivering; as if the weather had been cold.

June 20. No rest all night, violent pains in my head, and feverish.

June 21. Very ill, frightened almost to death at my sad condition, to be sick and no help. Prayed to God for the first time since the storm off Hull, but scarcely knew what I said, or why, my thoughts being all confused.

June 22. A little better, but with dreadful fears of sickness.

June 23. Very bad again, cold and shivering, and then a violent headache.

June 24. Much better.

June 25. A very violent ague; the fit held me seven hours, cold fit and hot, with faint sweats after it.

June 26. Better. Having no food to eat, I took

June 27. The ague again so violent that I lay abed all day, and neither ate nor drank. I was ready to perish for thirst, but so weak I had not strength to stand up, or to get myself any water to drink. I prayed to God again, but was lightheaded. When I was not, I was so ignorant that I knew not what to say. I lay and cried, "Lord, look upon me; Lord, pity me; Lord, have mercy upon me." I suppose I did nothing else for two or three hours, till, the fit wearing off, I fell asleep, and did not wake till far in the night. When I waked I found myself much refreshed, but weak and exceedingly thirsty. However, as I had no water in my whole place I was forced to lie till morning, and went to sleep again.

June 28. I was somewhat refreshed with the sleep I had had, and the fit had entirely passed off, so I got up. I thought that the ague would return again next day, and that now was my time to get something to refresh and support myself when I should be ill. The first thing I did was to fill a large, square case bottle with water, and set it upon my table, in reach of my bed. Then I got a piece of the goat's flesh, and broiled it on the coals, but could eat very little. I walked about, but was very weak, and withal, very sad and heavyhearted under a sense of my miserable condition, dreading the return of my distemper the

next day. At night I made my supper of three of
the turtle's eggs, which I roasted in the ashes, and ate,
as we call it, in the shell. This was the first bit of
meat I had ever asked God's blessing on, as I could
remember, in my whole life.

After I had eaten I tried to walk, but I found myself so weak that I could hardly carry the gun (for
I never went out without that). I went but a little
way, and sat down upon the ground, looking out
upon the sea, which was very calm and smooth.

After a time I arose, feeling very pensive and sad,
and walked back to my retreat. I went up over my
wall, as if I had been going to bed, but my thoughts
were sadly disturbed, and I had no inclination to
sleep, so I sat down in my chair, and lighted my lamp,
for it began to be dark. I took up the Bible, and
opened it casually. The first words that occurred to
me were these: "Call on me in the day of trouble,
and I will deliver thee, and thou shalt glorify me."

The words were very apt to my case, and made
some impression upon my thoughts at the time of
reading them, though not so much as they did afterward. As for being delivered, the word had no
sound, as I may say, to me; the thing was so remote,
so impossible in my apprehension of things, that I
began to say as the Children of Israel did when they
were promised flesh to eat, "Can God spread a table
in the wilderness?" So I began to say, "Can God
Himself deliver me from this place?" And as it was
not for many years that any hope appeared, this oc-

curred very often to my thoughts. However, the words made a very great impression upon me, and I mused upon them very often. It now grew late, and so I left my lamp burning in the cave, lest I should want anything in the night, and went to bed. Before I lay down, I did what I never had done in all my life; I knelt down and prayed to God to fulfill the promise to me, that if I called upon Him in the day of trouble, He would deliver me. After my broken and imperfect prayer was over, I went to bed, and fell into a sound sleep, and waked no more, till noon the next day. Nay, to this hour, I am partly of the opinion that I slept all the next day and night, and till almost three the day after; for otherwise I knew not how I should lose a day out of my reckoning in the days of the week, as it appeared some years after I had done. If I had lost it by crossing and re-crossing the line, I should have lost more than one day, but certainly I lost a day in my account, and never knew how.

At any rate, when I waked I found myself exceedingly refreshed, and my spirits lively and cheerful. When I got up I was stronger than I was the day before, and my stomach better, for I was hungry. In short, I had no fit the next day, but continued much better. This was the 29th.

The 30th was my well day, of course, and I went abroad with my gun, but did not care to travel too far. I killed a seafowl or two, something like a brand goose, and brought them home, but was not very eager to eat them, so I ate some more of the turtle's eggs, which were very good. However, I was not so well the next day, which was the first of July, as I hoped I should have been, for I had a little spell of the cold fit, but it was not much.

July 3. I did not have another fit, though I did not recover my full strength for some weeks after. While I was thus gathering strength, my thoughts ran exceedingly upon the Scripture, "I will deliver thee." The impossibility of my deliverance lay much upon my mind, to bar my ever expecting it, but as I was discouraging myself with such thoughts, it occurred to my mind that I poured so much on my deliverance from the main affliction, that I disregarded the deliverance I had received. I was, as it were, made to ask myself such questions as these:

"Have I not been delivered, and wonderfully, too, from sickness and from the most distressed condition that could be that was so frightful to me. What notice had I taken of it? Had I done my part? God had delivered me, but I had not glorified Him, that is to say, I had not owned and been thankful for that as a deliverance. How could I expect greater deliverance?"

This touched my heart very much, and immediately I knelt down and gave God thanks, aloud, for my recovery from my sickness.

July 4. In the morning I took the Bible and, beginning at the New Testament, I began seriously to read it, and imposed upon myself to read awhile every morning and every night, not tying myself to the number of chapters, but as long as my thoughts should engage me. It was not long after I set seriously to this work that I found my heart more deeply and sincerely affected with the wickedness of my past life.

Now I began to construe the words mentioned above, "Call on me, and I will deliver thee," in a different sense from what I had ever done before. Then I had no notion of anything being called deliverance, but my being delivered from the captivity I was in, for though I was indeed at large in the place, yet the island was certainly a prison to me, and that in the worst sense in the world. Now I learned to understand the words in another sense. I looked back upon my past life with such horror, and my sins appeared so dreadful, that my soul sought nothing of God but deliverance from the load of guilt that bore down all my comfort. As for my solitary life, it was nothing. I did not so much as pray to be delivered from it, or think of it. It was all of no consideration in comparison with this. And I add this part here, to hint to whomever shall read it, that whenever they come to a true sense of things, they will find deliverance from sin a much greater blessing than deliverance from affliction.

But, leaving this part, I returned to my Journal.

My condition began now to be, though not less miserable as to my way of living, yet much easier as to my mind. My thoughts were directed by a con-

stant reading of the Scripture and praying to God
to things of a higher nature. I had a great deal of
comfort within, which till now I knew nothing of.
Also, as my health and strength returned, I bestirred
myself to supply everything that I wanted, and make
my way of living as regular as I could.

From the 4th of July to the 14th, I was chiefly
employed in walking about with my gun in my hand,
a little at a time, as a man does who is gathering up
his strength after a fit of sickness, for it is hardly to
be imagined how low I was, and to what weakness
I was reduced.

I learned from it this, in particular, that being
abroad in the rainy season was the most injurious
thing to my health that could be, especially in those
rains which came attended with storms and hurri-
canes of wind. As the rain which came in the dry
season was always most accompanied with such
storms, so I found this rain was much more danger-
ous than the rain which fell in September and
October.

I had been now in this unhappy island above ten
months. All possibility of deliverance from this condition seemed to be entirely taken from me, and
I firmly believed that no human person had ever set
foot upon that place.

Making a Country Home ❧

SINCE I had now made my dwelling perfectly secure, as I thought, I had a great desire to make
a more complete investigation of the island, and to
see what other productions I might find, which I yet
knew nothing of.

It was on the 15th of July that I began to take a
more particular survey of the island itself; I went up
the creek first where, as I have said, I brought my
rafts on shore. I found, after I came about two
miles up, that the tide did not flow any higher, and
that it was no more than a little brook of running
water, very fresh and good. This was the dry season, and there was hardly any water in some parts of
it, at least not enough to run in any stream, so it
could be perceived.

On the banks of this brook I found many pleasant
meadows, plain, smooth, and covered with grass.
On the rising parts of them next to the higher
grounds, where the water, as it might be supposed,
never overflowed, I found a great deal of tobacco,

green, and growing to a great and very strong stalk. There were many other plants which I had no notion of or understanding about. They might perhaps have had virtues of their own, but I could not find out.

I searched for the cassava root, which the Indians in all that climate make their bread of, but I could not find any. I saw large plants of aloes, but did not then understand them. I saw several sugar canes, but wild, and, for want of cultivation, imperfect. I contented myself with these discoveries for this time, and came back musing with myself what course I might take to know the virtue and goodness of any of the fruits or plants which I should discover, but I could come to no conclusion. I had made so little observation while I was in the Brazils, that I knew little of the plants of the field, at least very little that might serve me to any purpose now in my distress.

The next day, the 16th, I went up the same way again, and, after going something farther, I found that the brook and the meadows began to cease, and the country became more woody. In this part I found different fruits, and particularly I found melons upon the ground in great abundance, and grapes upon the trees. The vines had spread indeed over the trees, and the clusters of grapes were just now in their prime, very ripe and rich. This was a surprising discovery, and I was exceedingly glad of them, but I was afraid to eat many of them. I found an excellent use for these grapes, however. That was

to cure or dry them in the sun and keep them as
dried grapes or raisins are kept, which I thought
would be, as indeed they were, as wholesome and as
agreeable to eat, when no grapes might be had.

I spent all that evening there, and did not go back
to my dwelling, which, by the way, was the first
night, as I might say, that I had slept away from
home. In the night I followed my first contrivance,
and got up into a tree, where I slept well. The next
morning I proceeded upon my discovery, traveling
nearly four miles, as I might judge by the length of
the valley, keeping still due north, with a ridge of
hills on the south and north side of me.

At the end of this walk I came to an opening,
where the country seemed to descend to the west.
A little spring of fresh water, which issued out of
the side of the hill by me, ran the other way, that is,
due east. The country appeared so fresh, so green,
so flourishing, everything being in a constant verdure
or flourishing of spring, that it looked like a planted
garden.

I descended a little on the side of that delicious
valley, surveying it with a secret kind of pleasure
(though mixed with other afflicting thoughts), to
think that this was all my own, that I was king and
lord of all this country indefeasibly, and had a right
of possession. If I could convey it, I might have it
in inheritance, as completely as any lord of a manor
in England. I saw here abundance of coconut trees,
orange and lemon and citron trees, but all wild, and

few bearing any fruit; at least not then. However, the green limes that I gathered were not only pleasant to eat, but very wholesome, and I mixed their juice afterward with water, which made it cool and refreshing.

I found now that I had fruit enough to gather and carry home. I resolved to lay up a store, as well of grapes as of limes and lemons, to furnish myself for the wet season, which I knew was approaching.

In order to do this I gathered a heap of grapes in one place, and a smaller heap in another place, and a great parcel of limes and lemons in another place. Taking a few of each with me, I traveled homeward, and resolved to come again and bring a bag or sack, or what I could make, to carry the rest home.

Accordingly, having spent three days in this journey, I came home (so I must now call my tent and my cave), but before I got thither the grapes were spoiled. The richness of the fruit and the weight of the juice had broken them and bruised them, and they were good for little or nothing. As to the limes, they were very good, but I could bring but a few.

The next day, being the 19th, I went back, having made two small bags to bring home my harvest. But I was surprised when, coming to my heap of grapes, which were so rich and fine when I gathered them, I found them all spread abroad, trod to pieces, and dragged about, some here, some there, and many eaten and devoured. By this I concluded that there were some wild creatures thereabouts which had done this, but what they were I knew not.

However, as I found that there was no laying them up on heaps, and no carrying them away in a sack, for one way they would be destroyed, and the other way they would be crushed with their own weight, I took another course. I gathered a large quantity of the grapes and hung them upon the outer branches of the trees, that they might cure and dry in the sun. As for the limes and lemons, I carried as many back as I could well stand under.

When I came home from this journey, I thought with great pleasure of the fruitfulness of that valley, and the pleasantness of the situation, the security from storms on that side of the water, and the wood, and I concluded that I had selected what was by far the worst part of the country for my abode. Upon the whole, I began to consider moving my dwelling, and looking out for a place as safe as where I now was situated, if possible, in that pleasant and fruitful part of the island.

This thought ran long in my head, and I was exceeding fond of it for some time, the pleasantness of the place tempting me. However, when I came to a nearer view of it, I considered that I was now by the seaside, where it was at least possible that something might happen to my advantage, and that the same ill fate that brought me hither, might bring some other unhappy wretches to the same place. Though it was scarcely probable that any such thing

should ever happen, yet to enclose myself among the hills and woods, in the center of the island, was to anticipate my bondage, and to render such an affair not only improbable, but impossible. Therefore, I decided that I ought not by any means to move.

However, I was so enamored of this place, that I spent much of my time there for the whole remaining part of the month of July, and though, upon second thoughts, I resolved as I said above, not to move, yet I built a kind of little bower, and surrounded it at a distance with a strong fence, a double hedge, as high as I could reach, well staked and filled between with brushwood. Here I lay very secure, sometimes two or three nights together, always going over it with a ladder, as before. I fancied that now I had my country house, and my seacoast house. This work took me up to the beginning of August.

I had but newly finished my fence, and begun to enjoy my labor, when the rains came on, and made me stick close to my first dwelling. Though at my country home I had made a tent like the other, with a piece of sail, and spread it very well, yet I had not the shelter of a hill to keep me from storms, nor a cave behind me to retreat into when the rains were heavy.

About the beginning of August, as I said, I had finished my bower, and begun to enjoy myself. The 3d of August I found that the grapes I had hung up were perfectly dried, and indeed were excellent sundried raisins. I began to take them down from the trees, and it was very fortunate that I did so, for the rains which followed would have spoiled them, and I should have lost the best part of my winter food. I had more than two hundred large bunches of them. No sooner had I taken them all down and carried most of them home to my cave, than it began to rain. From then, which was the 14th of August, it rained more or less every day till the middle of October, sometimes so violently that I could not stir out of my cave for several days.

In this season I was much surprised with the increase of my family. I had been concerned for the loss of one of my cats, who ran away from me, or, as I thought, had died, and I heard no more tidings of her, till, to my astonishment, she came home about the end of August, with three kittens. This was the more strange to me, because though I had killed a

wild cat, as I called it, with my gun, I thought it was
a quite different kind from our European cats, yet
the young cats were the same kind of house breed as
the old one.

From the 14th of August to the 26th the rain was
incessant, so that I could not stir, and was now very
careful not to be much wet. In this confinement I
began to be in need of food, but venturing out twice,
I one day killed a goat, and the last day, which was
the 26th, found a very large tortoise, which was a
treat to me. My food was regulated thus: I ate a
bunch of raisins for my breakfast, a piece of the
goat's flesh, or of the turtle, for my dinner, broiled
(for to my great misfortune I had no vessel to boil
or stew anything in), and two or three of the turtle's
eggs for supper.

During this confinement in my cover, by the rain,
I worked daily two or three hours at enlarging my
cave. By degrees, I worked it on toward one side,
till I came to the outside of the hill, and made a door
or way out, which came beyond my fence or wall.
So I came in and out this way. But I was not perfectly easy at lying so open, for as I had managed
myself before, I was in a perfect enclosure, whereas
now I thought I lay exposed. Yet I could not perceive that there was any living thing to fear, the biggest creature that I had seen upon the island being a
goat.

September 30. I was now come to the unhappy
anniversary of my landing. I counted up the notches

on my post, and found that I had been on shore three
hundred and sixty-five days. I kept this day as a
solemn fast, setting it apart to a religious exercise,
prostrating myself on the ground with the most serious humiliation, confessing my sins to God, ac-
knowledging His righteous judgments upon me, and
praying to Him to have mercy on me, through Jesus
Christ. I had not tasted the least refreshment for
twelve hours, even to the going down of the sun, and
I then ate a biscuit and a bunch of grapes, and went
to bed, finishing the day as I began it.

I had all this time observed no Sabbath Day, for
as at first I had no sense of religion upon my mind,
I had after some time omitted to distinguish the
weeks, by making a longer notch than ordinary for
the Sabbath Day, and so did not really know what
any of the days were. Now, having counted up the
days, I found that I had been there a year, so I divided
it into weeks, and set apart every seventh day for a
Sabbath, though I found at the end of my account
I had lost a day or two in my reckoning.

A little after this my ink began to fail me, and so
I contented myself to use it more sparingly, and to
write down only the most remarkable events of my
life, without continuing a daily memorandum of
other things.

The rainy season and the dry season began now
to appear regular to me, and I learned to divide them
so as to provide for them accordingly. But I bought
all my experience before I had it, and this that I am

going to relate was one of the most discouraging experiments that I made. I have mentioned that I had saved the few ears of barley and rice which I had so surprisingly found spring up, as I thought, of themselves. I believe that there were about thirty stalks of rice and about twenty of barley. I thought it a proper time to sow it after the rains, the sun being in its southern position.

Accordingly, I dug up a piece of ground, as well as I could, with my wooden spade, and dividing it into two parts, I sowed my grain, but as I was sowing, it casually occurred to my thought, that I would not sow it all at first, because I did not know when was the proper time for it, so I sowed about two-thirds of the seeds, leaving about a handful of each. It was a great comfort to me afterward that I did so, for not one grain of that which I sowed this time came to anything. The dry months followed, and since the earth had no rain after the seed was sown, the seed had no moisture to assist its growth, and never came up at all, till the wet season had come again, and then it grew as if it had been newly sown.

Finding that my first seed did not grow, which I easily imagined was by the drought, I sought for a moister piece of ground to make another trial in. I dug up a piece of ground near my new bower, and sowed the rest of my seed in February, a little before the vernal equinox. This had the rainy months of March and April to water it and sprang up very flourishingly and yielded a very good crop. How-

ever, since I had only part of the seed left, and did
not dare to sow all that I had, I had but a small quantity at last, my whole crop not amounting to more
than half a peck of each kind.

But by this experience I was made master of my
business, and knew exactly when the proper season
was to sow, and that I might expect two seedtimes
and two harvests every year.

While this grain was growing, I made a little discovery, which was of use to me afterward. As soon
as the rains were over and the weather began to settle,
which was about the month of November, I made
a visit up the country to my bower. I had not been
there for some months, but I found all things just as
I had left them. The circle or double hedge that I
had made was not only firm and entire, but the stakes
which I had cut off some trees that grew thereabouts
had budded and grown long branches, much as a
willow tree usually puts out shoots the first year after
it is cut back. I could not tell what tree to call it
that these stakes were cut from. I was surprised, and
yet very well pleased, to see the young trees grow.
I pruned them, and led them to grow as much alike
as I could, and it is scarcely credible how beautiful
a figure they grew into in three years. Though the
hedge made a circle of about twenty-five yards in
diameter, yet the trees, for such I might now call
them, soon covered it, and it was a complete shade,
sufficient to lodge under all the dry season.

This made me resolve to cut some more stakes, and

make me a hedge like this in a semicircle round the wall of my first dwelling, which I did. Placing the trees or stakes in a double row, at about eight yards' distance from my first fence, they grew presently, and were at first a fine cover to my habitation, and afterward served for a defense also, as I shall observe in its order.

I found now that the seasons of the year might generally be divided, not into summer and winter, as in Europe, but into the rainy seasons and the dry seasons, which were generally thus:

Half February, March, half April—Rainy, the sun being then on or near the equinox.

Half April, May, June, July, half August—Dry, the sun being then to the north of the line.

Half August, September, half October—Rainy, the sun then being come back.

Half October, November, December, January, half February—Dry, the sun being then to the south of the line.

The rainy season sometimes held longer or shorter, as the winds happened to blow, but this was the general observation I made. After I had found, by experience, the ill consequences of being abroad in the rain, I took care to furnish myself with provisions beforehand, that I might not be obliged to go out, and I sat within doors as much as possible during the wet months.

In this time I found much employment (and very suitable also to the time), for I found great occasion for many things which I had no way to furnish myself with, but by hard labor and constant application. I employed myself in making (as well as I could) a great many baskets, both to carry earth, or to carry or lay up anything, as I had occasion. Though I did not finish them very handsomely, yet I made them sufficiently serviceable for my purpose. After that I took care never to be without them, and as my wickerware decayed, I made more. I made strong, deep baskets to place my grain in, when I should come to have any quantity of it.

Having mastered this difficulty, and employed a world of time about it, I bestirred myself to see, if possible, how to supply two wants. I had no vessels to hold anything that was liquid, except two runlets, which were almost full of rum, and some glass bottles, some of the common size, and others, which were case bottles, square, for the holding of water and spirits. I had not so much as a pot to boil anything in, except a great kettle which I saved out of the ship, and which was too big for such uses as I desired for it, namely, to make broth, and stew a bit of meat by itself. The second thing I wanted was a tobacco pipe, but it was impossible for me to make one. However, I found a contrivance for that, too, at last.

Ten Years of Work 〰

I MENTIONED before that I had a great mind to see the whole island, and that I had traveled up the brook and so on to where I had built my bower, and where I had an opening quite to the sea, on the other side of the island. I now resolved to travel quite across to the seashore on that side, so, taking my gun and my hatchet and my dog and a larger quantity of powder and shot than usual, with two biscuit cakes and a great bunch of raisins in my pouch for my store, I began my journey. When I had passed the vale where my bower stood, I came within view of the sea, to the west. It was a very clear day, and I could see land, though whether it was an island or a continent I could not tell. It lay very high, extending from the west to the WSW. at a very great distance. By my guess it could not be less than fifteen or twenty leagues off.

I could not tell what part of the world this might be, otherwise than that I knew it must be part of America, and, as I concluded by all my observations,

must be near the Spanish dominions, and perhaps was
all inhabited by savages, where, if I should have landed,
I had been in a worse condition than I was now.
Therefore, I acquiesced in the dispositions of Providence, which I began now to own, and to believe,
ordered everything for the best. I say I quieted my
mind with this, and stopped afflicting myself with
fruitless wishes of being there.

Besides, after some pause upon this affair, I considered that if this land was the Spanish coast, I should
certainly, one time or other, see some vessel pass or
repass. If it was not, then it was the savage coast
between the Spanish country and Brazil, which is inhabited by the worst of savages, for they are cannibals,
or meneaters, and fail not to murder and devour all
the human bodies that fall into their hands.

With these considerations I walked very leisurely
forward. I found that side of the island where I now
was much pleasanter than mine, the open fields sweet,
adorned with flowers and grass, and full of very fine
woods. I saw abundance of parrots, and fain would
I have caught one, if possible, to have kept it to be
tame, and taught it to speak to me. I did, after some
pains taken, catch a young parrot, for I knocked him
down with a stick, and, having revived him, I brought
him home, but it was some years before I could make
him speak. However, at last I taught him to call me
by my name.

I was exceedingly diverted with this journey. I
found in the low grounds hares, as I thought them to

be, and foxes, but they differed greatly from all other kinds I had met with, nor could I bring myself to eat them, for I had no want of food, and of that which was very good; especially these three sorts, goats, pigeons, and turtle or tortoise. I had great cause for thankfulness that I was not driven to any extremities for food, but had plenty, even to dainties.

I never traveled in this journey more than two miles outright in a day, or thereabouts, but I took so many turns and returns, to see what discoveries I could make, that I came weary enough to the place where I resolved to spend the night. Then either I reposed myself in a tree, or surrounded myself with a row of stakes set upright in the ground, either from one tree or another, so that no wild creature could come at me without waking me.

As soon as I came to the seashore, I was surprised to see that I had taken up my lot on the worst side of the island, for here indeed the shore was covered with innumerable turtles, whereas, on the other side I had found but three in a year and a half. Here was also an infinite number of fowls of many kinds, some of which I had not seen before, and many of them very good meat, but such as I knew not the names of, except those called penguins.

I could have shot as many as I pleased, but I was very sparing of my powder and shot, and therefore had more mind to kill a she-goat, if I could, which I could better feed on. Though there were many more goats here than on the other side of the island, yet it was with much more difficulty that I could come near them, the country being flat and even, so that they saw me much sooner than when I was on the hills.

I confess this side of the country was much pleasanter than mine, but yet I had not the least inclination to move, for, as I was fixed in my habitation, it became natural to me. I seemed all the while I was here to be, as it were, upon a journey and from home. However, I traveled along the shore of the sea toward the east, I suppose about twelve miles, and then, setting up a great pole upon the shore for a mark, I concluded that

I would go home again. The next journey I planned to take on the other side of the island, east from my dwelling, and so round, till I came to my post again, of which in its place.

I took another way to come back than that I went, thinking I could easily keep all the island so much in my view, that I could not miss finding my first dwelling by viewing the country, but I found myself mistaken. When I had gone about two or three miles, I found myself descended into a very large valley, so surrounded with hills, and those hills so covered with woods, that I could not see which was my way by any direction but that of the sun.

It happened that the weather proved hazy for three or four days while I was in this valley, and, not being able to see the sun, I wandered about very uncomfortably, and at last was obliged to find out the seaside, look for my post, and come back the same way I went. Then by easy journeys I turned homeward, the weather being exceedingly hot, and my gun, ammunition, hatchet, and other things very heavy.

In this journey my dog surprised a young kid and seized upon it. I, running to take hold of it, caught it, and saved it alive from the dog. I had a great mind to bring it home, if I could, for I had often been musing whether it might not be possible to get a kid or two, and so raise a breed of tame goats, which might supply me when my powder and shot should be spent.

I made a collar for this little creature, and with a string which I made of some rope yarn, which I always carried about me, I led him along, though with some difficulty, till I came to my bower. There I enclosed him, and left him, for I was very impatient to be at home, from whence I had been absent more than a month.

I cannot express what a satisfaction it was to me to come into my old hutch and lie down in my hammock bed. This little wandering journey, without a settled place of abode, had been so unpleasant to me that my own house, as I called it to myself, was a perfect settlement to me, compared to that. It made everything about me so comfortable that I resolved that I would never go a great way from it again, while it should be my lot to stay on the island.

I reposed myself here a week, to rest and regale myself after my long journey. Most of this time was taken up in the weighty affair of making a cage for my Poll, who began now to be tame and to be mighty well acquainted with me. Then I began to think of the poor kid, which I had shut in within my little circle, and resolved to go and bring it home, and give it some food. Accordingly, I went and found it where I had left it; for indeed it could not get out, but was almost starved for want of food. I went and cut boughs of trees and branches of such shrubs as I could find, and threw over to it. When I had fed it, I tied it as I did before to lead it away, but it was so tamewithbeing hungry, that I had no need to have tied it, for it followed me like a dog. As I continually fed it, the creature became so loving, so gentle, and so fond, that it became from that time one of my pets, also, and would never leave me afterward.

The rainy season of the autumnal equinox was now come, and I kept the 30th of September in the same solemn manner as before, it being the anniversary of my landing on the island. I had now been there two years, and had no more prospect of being delivered than I had the first day I came there. I spent the whole day in humble and thankful acknowledgments of the many wonderful mercies which my solitary condition was attended with, and without which it might have been infinitely more miserable. I gave humble and hearty thanks that God has been pleased to show me that it was possible for me to be happier in this solitary condition than I should have been in society, and in all the pleasures of the world.

I never opened the Bible or shut it, but my very soul within me blessed God for directing my friend in England, without any order of mine, to pack it among my goods, and for assisting me afterward to save it out of the wreck of the ship.

In this frame of mind, I began my third year. Though I have not given the reader the trouble of so particular an account of my works this year as at the first, yet in general it may be observed that I was very seldom idle. I regularly divided my time according to the several daily employments that were before me, such as: first, my duty to God, and reading the Scriptures, which I constantly set apart some time for, thrice every day; second, the going abroad with my gun for food, which generally took me about three hours every morning when it did not rain; third, the ordering, curing, preserving, and cooking what I had killed or caught for my supply. These took up a great part of the day. Also, it is to be considered that in the middle of the day, the intensity of the heat was too great for me to stir out, so that about four hours in the evening was all the time I could be supposed to work in. Sometimes I changed my hours of hunting and working, and went to work in the morning, and abroad with my gun in the afternoon.

To this short time allowed for labor I desire may be added the exceeding laboriousness of my work and the many hours which, for want of tools, want of help, and want of skill, everything that I did took up out of my time. For example, I was full two-and-forty days making me a board for a long shelf, which I wanted in my cave; whereas two sawyers, with their tools and saw pit, would have cut six of them out of the same tree in a half day.

My case was this: It was to be a large tree which was to be cut down, because my board was to be a broad one. I was three days cutting down the tree and two more cutting off the boughs, and reducing it to a log, or piece of timber. With inexpressible hacking and hewing, I reduced both the sides of it into chips, till it began to be light enough to move. Then I turned it, and made one side of it smooth and flat as a board, from end to end, then turning that side downward, I cut the other side till I made the plank about three inches thick, and smooth on both sides. Anyone may judge the labor of my hands in such a piece of work; but labor and patience carried me through that and many other things.

I was now in the months of November and December, expecting my crop of barley and rice. The ground I had manured or dug up for them was not great, for, as I observed, my seed of each was not above the quantity of half a peck, for I had lost one whole crop by sowing in the dry season. Now my crop promised very well, when I found I was in danger of losing it all again by enemies of several sorts, which it was scarcely possible to keep from it. At first, the goats and wild creatures whch I called hares, tasting the sweetness of the blade, lay in it night and day, as soon as it came up, and ate it so close, that it could get no time to shoot up into stalks.

This I saw no remedy for but by making an enclosure about it with a hedge, which I did with a great deal of toil and the more, because it required a great deal of speed, for the creatures were daily spoiling my grain. However, as my arable land was but small, suited to my crop, I got it totally well fenced in about three weeks' time. Shooting some of the creatures in the daytime, I set my dog to guard it in the night, tying him up to a stake at the gate, where he would stand and bark all night long. So, in a little time the enemies forsook the place, and the grain grew very strong and well, and began to ripen apace.

But as the beasts almost ruined me before, while my

grain was in the blade, so the birds came near ruin-
ing me now, when it was in the ear. Going along by
the place to see how it throve, I saw my little crop surrounded with fowls of I know not how many sorts,
which stood as it were watching till I should be gone.
I immediately let fly among them (for I always had
my gun with me). I had no sooner shot, but there
arose up a little cloud of fowls, which I had not seen at
all, from among the corn itself.

I foresaw that in a few days they would devour all
my hopes. I should be starved, and never be able to

raise a crop at all, and what to do I could not tell. However, I resolved not to lose my grain if possible, though I should watch it night and day. In the first place, I went among it to see what damage was already done, and found that they had spoiled a good deal of it, but that, as it was yet too green for them, the loss was not so great. The remainder was likely to be a good crop, if it could be saved.

I stayed by it to load my gun, and then coming away, I could easily see the thieves sitting upon all the trees about me, as if they waited only till I was gone away. The event proved it to be so, for as I walked off, as if I were gone, I was no sooner out of their sight, than they dropped down one by one into the grain again. I was so provoked, that I could not have patience to stay till more came on, knowing that every grain that they ate now was, as it might be said, a peck loaf to me in the consequence. Coming up to the hedge, I fired again, and killed three of them. This was what I wished for, so I took them up, and served them, as we serve notorious thieves in England, that is, hanged them in chains, for a terror to others. It is almost impossible to imagine that this should have such an effect as it had, for the fowls would not only not come at the grain, but in short they forsook all that part of the island, and I could never see a bird near the place as long as my scarecrows hung there. This I was very glad of, you may be sure, and about the latter end of December, which was our second harvest of the year, I reaped my grain.

I was sadly put to it for a scythe or a sickle to cut
it down, and all I could do was to make one as well as
I could, out of one of the broadswords, or cutlasses,
which I saved among the arms out of the ship. However, as my crop was but small, I had no great difficulty in cutting it down. I reaped it my way, for I
cut nothing off but the ears, and carried it away in a
great basket which I had made, and so rubbed it out
with my hands. At the end of all my harvesting I
found that out of my half peck of seed, I had nearly
two bushels of rice, and more than two bushels and a
half of barley, that is to say, by my guess, for I had
no measure at that time.

However, this was a great encouragement to me,
and I foresaw that in time it would please God to
supply me with bread. Yet here I was perplexed
again, for I neither knew how to grind or make meal
of my grain, or indeed how to clean it and separate it;
nor, if it was made into meal, how to make bread of it,
and if I found out how to make it, yet I knew not how
to bake it. These things being added to my desire of
having a good quantity for store, and of securing a
constant supply, I resolved not to taste any of this
crop, but to preserve it all for seed against the next
season, and in the meantime to employ all my study
and hours of working to accomplish this great work
of providing myself with grain and bread.

It might be truly said that now I worked for my
bread. It is a little wonderful to consider, as I believe
few people do, the strange multitude of little things

necessary in the providing, producing, curing, dressing, making, and finishing this one article, bread.

First, I had no plow to turn the earth, no spade or shovel to dig it. Well, this I conquered by making a wooden spade, as I observed before, but this did my work in but a wooden manner. Though it cost me a great many days to make it, yet, for want of iron, it not only wore out the sooner, but made my work the harder, and made it be performed much worse.

However, this I bore with, too, and was content to work it out with patience, and bear with the badness of the performance. When the grain was sown, I had no harrow, but was forced to go over the ground myself, and drag a great heavy bough of a tree over it, to scratch the earth, as it may be called, rather than rake or harrow it.

When it was growing or grown, I have observed already how many things I wanted, to fence it, secure it, mow or reap it, cure or carry it home, thresh, separate it from the chaff, and save it. Then I wanted a mill to grind it, sieves to dress it, yeast and salt to make it into bread, and an oven to bake it in. All these things I did without, as shall be observed; yet the grain was an inestimable comfort and advantage to me, too. But all this, as I said, made everything laborious and tedious to me, but that there was no help for, neither was my time so much loss to me, because I had divided it. A certain part of it was every day appointed to these works, and as I resolved to use none of the grain for bread till I had a greater quantity by me, I had the next six months to apply myself, wholly by labor and invention, to furnish myself with utensils proper for performing all the operations necessary for making the grain, when I had it, fit for my use.

But first I had to prepare more land, for I had now seed enough to sow more than an acre of ground. Before I did this, I had a week's work at least to make a spade, which, when it was done, was a very sorry one indeed, and very heavy, and required double labor to work with it. However, I went through that, and sowed my seeds in two large, flat pieces of ground, as near my house as I could find them to suit me, and fenced them in with a good hedge, the stakes of which were all cut off that wood which I had set before, which I knew would grow. In one year's time I knew I should have a quick or living hedge, that would want but little repair. This work was not so little as to take me up less than three months; because a great part of that time was in the wet season, when I could not go abroad.

Within doors, when it rained and I could not go out I found employment, always observing, that all the while I was at work, I diverted myself with talking to my parrot, and teaching him to speak. I quickly taught him to know his own name, "Poll," or at least, to speak it out pretty loud. This was the first word I ever heard spoken in the island by any mouth but my own.

I had long studied, by some means or other, to make myself some earthen vessels, which indeed I wanted sorely, but knew not where to get them. However, considering the heat of the climate, I did not doubt that if I could find any clay, I might botch up some such pot, as might, being dried by the sun, be hard enough and strong enough to bear handling, and to hold anything that was dry and required to be kept so. As this was necessary in preparing meal, which was the thing I was upon, I resolved to make some as large as I could, and fit only to stand like jars to hold what should be put into them.

It would make the reader pity me, or rather laugh at me, to hear how many awkward ways I took to raise this paste, what odd, misshapen, ugly things I made, how many of them fell in, and how many fell out, the clay not being stiff enough to bear its own weight; how many cracked by the overviolent heat of the sun, being set out too hastily; how many fell to pieces when they were moved, as well before as after they were dried. In a word, after having labored hard to find the clay, to dig it, to temper it, to bring it home, and work it, I could not make more than two large, earthen, ugly things, I cannot call them jars, in about two months' labor.

However, as the sun baked these two very dry and hard, I lifted them very gently up, and set them down again in two great wicker baskets, which I had made on purpose for them, that they might not break, and, as between the pot and the basket there was a little room to spare, I stuffed it full of the rice and barley straw. I thought that these two pots would hold my dry grain, and perhaps the meal when the grain was bruised.

Though I miscarried so much in my design for large pots, yet I made several smaller things with better success, such as little round pots, flat dishes, pitchers, and pipkins, and anything my hand turned to, and the heat of the sun baked them strangely hard.

But all this would not answer my end, which was to get an earthen pot to hold what was liquid, and bear the fire, which none of these could do. It happened after some time that I made a pretty large fire for cooking my meat. When I went to put it out after I had done with it, I found a broken piece of one of my earthenware vessels in the fire, burned as hard as a stone and red as a tile. I was agreeably surprised to see it, and said to myself that certainly they might be made to burn whole, if they would burn broken.

This set me to study how to order my fire, so as to make it burn me some pots. I had no notion of a kiln, such as the potters burn in, or of glazing them with lead, though I had some lead to do it with, but I placed three large pipkins and two or three pots in a pile one upon another, and placed my firewood all round it, with a great heap of embers under them. I plied the fire with fresh fuel round the outside and upon the top, till I saw the pots in the inside red-hot quite through, and observed that they did not crack at all. When I saw them clear red, I let them stand in that heat about five or six hours, till I found that one of them, though it did not crack, did melt or run. For the sand which was mixed with the clay, melted by the violence of the heat and would have run into glass, if I had gone on; so I slacked my fire gradually, till the red color of the pots began to fade. I watched them all night that I might not let the fire abate too fast, and in the morning I had three very good, I will not say handsome, pipkins, and two other earthen pots, as hard burned as could be desired, and one of them perfectly glazed with the running of the sand.

No joy at a thing of so mean a nature was ever equal to mine, when I found I had made earthen pots that would bear the fire. I had hardly patience to wait till they were cold, before I set one upon the fire again, with some water in it, to boil me some meat, which it did admirably well. With a piece of a kid I made some very good broth, though I lacked oatmeal and several other ingredients requisite to make it as good as I would have had it.

My next concern was to get me a stone mortar to stamp or beat some grain in. As to the mill, there was no thought of arriving to that perfection of art with one pair of hands. To supply this want, I was at a great loss, for of all trades in the world I was as perfectly unqualified for a stonecutter as for any. Neither had I any tools to go about it with. I spent many a day trying to find a great stone big enough to cut hollow and make fit for a mortar, and could find none at all. After a great deal of time lost in searching for a stone, I gave it up, and resolved to look for a great block of hard wood, which I found indeed much

easier. Getting one as big as I had strength to stir, I
rounded it, and formed it on the outside with my ax
and hatchet. Then, with the help of fire and infinite
labor, I made a hollow place in it, as the Indians in
Brazil make their canoes. After this, I made a great
heavy pestle or beater, of the wood called the iron-
wood. This I prepared and laid by against the time I
had my next crop of grain, when I proposed to myself
to grind, or rather pound, my grain or meal to make it
bread.

My next difficulty was to make a sieve, to dress my
meal and part it from the bran and the husk, without
which I did not see it possible I could have bread. At
last I remembered some seamen's clothing, some sails
of the ship, and some neckcloths of calico or muslin.
With some pieces of these I made three sieves, small,
but large enough for the work. Thus I made shift for
some years.

The baking part was the next thing to be considered,
and how I should make bread when I came to have
grain, for, first, I had no yeast. As to that part, as
there was no supplying the want, I did not concern
myself much about it. But for an oven, I was indeed
at a loss. At length I made an experiment for that also,
which was this: I made some earthen vessels very
broad, but not deep; that is to say, about two feet in
diameter, and not more than nine inches deep. These
I burned in the fire, as I had done the others, and laid
them by. When I wanted to bake, I made a great fire
upon the hearth, which I had paved with some square

tiles of my own making and burning, also, but I should
not call them square. When the firewood was burned
pretty much into embers, or live coals, I drew the embers forward upon this hearth, so as to cover it all
over. There I let them lie, till the hearth was very
hot. Then sweeping away all the embers, I set down
my loaf, or loaves, and covered them with the earthen
pot. Then I drew the embers all round the outside
of the pot, to keep in and add to the heat. Thus, as
well as in the best oven in the world, I baked my
barley loaves, and became in a little time a pastry
cook into the bargain, for I made myself several cakes
and puddings of the rice.

It need not be wondered at if all these things took
me up most of the third year of my abode here, for it
must be remembered that in the intervals of these
things, I had my new harvest and husbandry to manage. I reaped my grain in its season and carried it
home as well as I could and laid it up in the ear, in my
large baskets, till I had time to rub it out, for I had no
floor to thrash it on, or instrument to thrash it with.

And now, indeed, my stock of grain increased and
I really wanted to build my barns bigger. I wanted
a place to lay it up in, for the increase of the grain now
yielded me so much that I had of the barley about
twenty bushels, and of the rice as much, or more. I
now resolved to begin to use it freely, for my bread
had been quite gone a great while, also I resolved to
see what quantity would be sufficient for me a whole
year, and to sow but once a year.

Upon the whole, I found that the forty bushels of
barley and rice were much more than I could consume
in a year, so I resolved to sow just the same quantity
every year that I sowed the last, in hopes that such a
quantity would fully provide me with bread.

All the while these things were doing, you may be
sure that my thoughts ran many times upon the prospect of land which I had seen from the other side of
the island.   I was not without secret wishes that I was
on shore there, fancying that seeing the mainland and
an inhabited country, I might find some way or other
to convey myself farther, and perhaps at last find
some means of escape.

But all this while I made no allowance for the dangers of such a condition, and how I might fall into the
hands of savages, and perhaps such as I might have
reason to think far worse than the lions and tigers of
Africa.   If I once came into their power, I should
run a hazard more than a thousand to one of being
killed, and perhaps of being eaten, for I had heard
that the people of the Caribbean coast were cannibals,
or meneaters, and I knew by the latitude that I could
not be far from that shore.   All these things, I say,
which I ought to have considered well, and which I
did cast up in my thoughts afterward, yet aroused
none of my apprehensions at first.   My mind ran
mightily upon the thoughts of getting over to that
shore.

At last I thought I would go and look at our ship's
boat.   She was blown up upon the shore a great way

in the storm, when we were first cast away. She lay almost where she did at first, but not quite, and was turned, by the force of the waves and the winds, almost bottom upward, against a high ridge of rough sand, but there was water about her as before.

But I was unable to move it, so I was forced to give it up. Yet, though I gave up hopes of the boat, my desire to venture over increased in the main, rather than decreased, as the means for it seemed impossible.

This at length set me to thinking whether it was not possible to make myself a canoe or periagua, such as the natives of those climates make, even without tools, of the trunk of a great tree. This I not only thought possible, but easy, and pleased myself extremely with my thoughts of making it, and with my having much more convenience for it than any of the Negroes or Indians. However, I did not at all consider the particular inconvenience which I lay under more than the Indians did, that is, the want of hands to move it into the water, when it was made. This was a difficulty much harder for me to surmount than all the consequences of want of tools could be to them. But my thoughts were so intent upon my voyage over the sea in it, that I never once considered how I should get it off the land. It was really in its own nature easier for me to guide it over forty-five miles of sea than over forty-five fathom of land, from where it lay, to set it afloat.

I went to work upon this boat and pleased myself with the plan, without determining whether I was able

to undertake it. The difficulty of launching my boat
came often into my head, but I put a stop to my own
inquiries into it by this foolish answer which I gave
myself: "Let me first make it, I will warrant I will
find some way or other to get it along when it is
done."

This was a most preposterous method, but the
eagerness of my fancy prevailed, and to work I went,
and felled a cedar tree. I question much whether
Solomon ever had such a one for building the Temple
of Jerusalem. It was five feet, ten inches in diameter
at the lower part next the stump, and four feet, eleven
inches in diameter at the end of twenty-two feet, after
which it lessened for a while and then parted into
branches. It was not without infinite labor that I
felled this tree; I was twenty days hacking and hewing at it at the bottom; I was fourteen more getting the
branches and limbs and the vast spreading head of it
cut off, which I hacked and hewed through with my
ax and hatchet, with inexpressible labor. After this it
cost me a month to shape it and rub it to a proportion,
and to something like the bottom of a boat, that it
might swim upright as it ought. It cost me nearly
three months more to clear the inside and work it out
so as to make an exact boat of it. This I did indeed
without fire, by mere mallet and chisel, and by the
dint of hard labor, till I had made it into a very handsome periagua, big enough to have carried six and
twenty men, and consequently big enough to have
carried me and all my cargo.

The boat was really much bigger than I had ever in my life seen a canoe or periagua that was made of one tree. Many a weary stroke it had cost, you may be sure, and now there remained nothing but to get it into the water. Had I succeeded in this, I make no question but I should have begun the maddest voyage, and the most unlikely to be performed, that ever was undertaken.

But all my devices to get the boat into the water failed me, though they cost infinite labor, too, for I could no more stir the canoe than I could the other boat. At length, though with great reluctance, I gave this attempt up also.

In the middle of this work I finished my fourth year in this place, and kept my anniversary with the same devotion, and with as much comfort, as ever before. By a constant study and serious application of the Word of God, and by the assistance of His grace, I had gained a different knowledge from that I had had before. I entertained different notions of things. I looked now upon the world as a thing remote, which I had nothing to do with, no expectation from, and indeed no desires about. In a word, I had nothing indeed to do with it, nor was likely to have, so I thought it looked, as we may perhaps look upon it hereafter, as a place I had lived in, but was come out of. And well might I say, as Father Abraham to Dives, "Between me and thee there is a great gulf fixed."

In the first place, I was removed from all the

wickedness of the world here. I had neither the lust of the flesh, the lust of the eye, nor the pride of life. I had nothing to covet, for I had all I was now capable of enjoying. I was lord of the manor, or, if I pleased, I might call myself king or emperor over the whole country which I had possession of; there were no rivals. I might have raised shiploads of grain, but I had no use for it; so I let as little grow as I thought enough for my occasion. I had tortoises or turtles enough, but one now and then was as much as I could put to any use. I had timber enough to have built a fleet of ships; I had grapes enough to have made wine, or to have cured into raisins, to have loaded that fleet when it had been built.

I had, as I hinted before, a parcel of money, as well gold as silver, about thirty-six pounds sterling. Alas, there the nasty, sorry, useless stuff lay! I had no use for it, and I often thought with myself that I would have given a handful of it for a gross of tobacco pipes, or for a handmill to grind my corn. Nay, I would have given it all for six-penny worth of turnip and carrot seed out of England, or for a handful of peas and beans, and a bottle of ink.

I had now been here so long that many things which I brought on shore for my help were either quite gone, or very much wasted, and nearly spent. My ink, as I observed, had been gone for some time, all but a very little, which I eked out with water a little and a little, till it was so pale it scarcely left any appearance of black upon the paper. As long as it lasted, I made use of it to mark down the days of the month on which any remarkable thing happened to me, and first, by casting up times past, I remembered that there was a strange concurrence of days, in the various fates which befell me, and which, if I had been superstitiously inclined to observe days as fatal or fortunate, I might have had reason to have looked upon with a great deal of curiosity.

First, I had observed that on the anniversary of the day that I broke away from my father and my friends and ran away to Hull in order to go to sea, the same day afterward I was taken by the Sallee man-of-war and made a slave.

One year from the very day that I escaped out of the wreck of that ship in Yarmouth Roads, I made my escape from Sallee in the boat.

The 30th of September, on my twenty-sixth birthday, I had my life miraculously saved when I was cast on shore on this island, so that my wicked life and my solitary life both began on the same day.

The next thing to give out after my ink were the biscuits which I had brought out of the ship. This I had husbanded to the last degree, allowing myself but one piece of bread a day for more than a year, and yet I was quite without bread for nearly a year before I got any grain of my own. Great reason I had to be thankful, too, that I had any at all, for getting it was, as has been already observed, next to miraculous.

My clothes, too, began to decay mightily. I had had no linen for a great while, except some checkered shirts which I found in the chests of the other seamen, and which I carefully preserved, because many times I could bear no clothes on but a shirt. It was a very great help to me that I had among all the men's clothes of the ship almost three dozen shirts. There were also several thick watch coats of the seamen's, but they were too hot to wear. Though it is true that the weather was so violently hot that there was no need of clothes, yet I could not go quite naked; nor could I bear the thought of it, though I was all alone.

One reason why I could not go quite naked was that I could not bear the heat of the sun so well when quite naked as with some clothes on. The very heat frequently blistered my skin, whereas, if I had a shirt on, the air itself made some motion, and whistling under the shirt, made me twofold cooler than I should have been without it. No more could I ever bring myself to go out in the heat of the sun without a cap or a hat. The heat of the sun beating with such violence as it does in that place, would give me the headache presently, so that I could not bear it; whereas, if I put on my hat, it would presently go away.

As I thought these things over, I began to consider about putting the few rags I had, which I called clothes, into some order. I had worn out all the waistcoats I had, and my business was now to try to make jackets out of the great watch coats which I had by me, and with such other materials as I had. Accordingly, I set to work tailoring, or rather, indeed, botching, for I made most piteous work of it. However, I made shift to make two or three waistcoats, which I hoped would serve me a great while. As for breeches or drawers, I made but a very sorry shift indeed till afterward.

I have mentioned that I saved the skins of all animals that I killed. I hung them up stretched out with sticks in the sun, by which means some of them were so dry and hard that they were fit for little, but others, it seems, were very useful. The first thing I made of these was a great cap for my head, with the hair on the outside to shoot off the rain. I did this so well that after this I made a suit of clothes wholly of those skins, that is to say, a waistcoat and breeches open at the knees, both loose, for they were rather wanted to keep me cool than to keep me warm. I must not omit to acknowledge that they were wretchedly made, for if I was a bad carpenter, I was a worse tailor. However, they were such as I made very good shift with, and when I was abroad, if it happened to rain, the hair of the waistcoat and cap being outmost, I was kept very dry.

After this I spent a deal of time and pains to make me an umbrella. I was indeed in great want of one, and had a great mind to make one. I had seen them made in the Brazils, where they are very useful in the great heat which is there. I felt the heat every jot as great here, and greater too, being nearer the equinox. Besides, as I was obliged to be much abroad, it was a most useful thing to me, as well for the rains as the heat. I took a world of pains at it, and was a great while before I could make anything likely to hold. Indeed, after I thought I had hit the way, I spoiled two or three before I made one to my mind, but at last I made one that answered indifferently well. The main difficulty I found was to make it let down. I could make it to spread, but if it did not let down, too, and draw in, it would not be portable for me anyway, but just over my head, which would not do. However, at last, as I said, I made one to answer. I covered it with skins, the hair upward, so that it cast off the rain like a penthouse, and kept off the sun so effectually that I could walk out in the hottest of the weather, with greater advantage than I could before in the coolest. When I had no need of it, I could close it, and carry it under my arm.

Thus I lived mighty comfortably, my mind being entirely composed by resigning to the will of God and throwing myself wholly upon the disposal of His providence.

I cannot say that after this, for five years, any extraordinary thing happened to me, but I lived on in the same course, in the same place, just as before. I had my yearly labor of planting my barley and rice and curing my raisins, of which I always kept just enough to have sufficient stock of the year's provisions beforehand. Besides these I undertook the task of making my daily labor of going out with my gun. I had, too, a canoe, which at last I finished. By digging a canal to it six feet wide and four feet deep, I brought it into the creek, almost half a mile away.

However, though my little periagua was finished, yet the size of it was not at all sufficient for the design which I had in view, when I made the first. I had planned to venture over to the land which I had seen, where it was more than forty miles broad. Accordingly, the smallness of my boat assisted to put an end to that design, and now I thought no more of it. But as I had a boat, my next design was to make a tour round the island. I had been on the other side, in one place, crossing, as I have already described it, over the land, and the discoveries that I had made in that journey had made me very eager to see other parts of the coast. Now that I had a boat, I thought of nothing but sailing round the island.

For this purpose, and that I might do everything with discretion and consideration, I fitted up a little mast to my boat, and made a sail to it out of some of the pieces of the ship's sails, of which I had a great store by me.

Having fitted my mast and sail and tried the boat, I found that she would sail very well. Then I made little lockers and boxes at each end of my boat, to put provisions, necessaries, and ammunition into, to be kept dry, either from rain or the spray of the sea. I cut a little, long hollow place in the inside of the boat, where I could lay my gun, making a flap to hang down over it to keep it dry.

I fixed my umbrella also in a step at the stern, like a mast, to stand over my head, and keep the heat of the sun off me, like an awning. Thus I every now and then took a little voyage upon the sea, but never went far out, nor far from the little creek. But at last, being eager to view the circumference of my little kingdom, I resolved upon my tour, and accordingly I supplied my ship with food for the voyage, putting in two dozen of my loaves (cakes I should rather call them) of barley bread, an earthen pot full of parched rice, a food I ate a great deal of, a little bottle of rum, half a goat, and powder with shot for killing more, and two large watch coats, which I took, one to lie upon, and the other to cover me in the night.

It was the sixth of November, in the sixth year of my reign, or my captivity, whichever you please, that I set out on this voyage. I found it much longer than I expected, for though the island itself was not very large, yet when I came to the east side to it, I found that a great ledge of rocks lay out about two leagues into the sea, some above water, some under it. Beyond this there was a shoal of sand, lying dry half a league more, so that I was obliged to go a great way out to sea to double that point.

When I first discovered them, I was going to give up my attempt and come back again, not knowing how far it might oblige me to go out to sea, and, above all, doubting how I should get back again. Accordingly I came to anchor, for I had made me a kind of anchor, with a piece of broken grappling which I got out of the ship.

Having secured my boat, I took my gun and went

on shore, climbing up a hill, which seemed to over-look that point, where I saw the full extent of it.

In my viewing the sea from that hill where I stood, I perceived a strong, and indeed, a most furious cur-rent, which ran to the east, and even came close to the point. I took the more notice of it, because I saw that there might be some danger that when I came into it, I might be carried out to sea by the strength of it, and not be able to make the island again. And, indeed, had I not gotten first upon this hill, I believe it would have been so, for there was the same current on the other side of the island, only that it set it off at a farther distance. I saw that there was a strong eddy under the shore, so I had nothing to do but to get out of the first current, and I should presently be in an eddy.

I lay here, however, two days, because the wind blowing pretty fresh (E. at SE. and that being just contrary to the current) made a heavy surf upon the point, so that it was not safe for me to keep too close to the shore on account of the surf, nor to go too far off because of the current.

The third day in the morning, the wind having abated overnight, the sea was calm, and I ventured, but I am a warning example again to all rash and ignorant pilots. No sooner was I come to the point, when I was not my boat's length from the shore, but I found myself in a great depth of water, and a current like the sluice of a mill. It carried my boat along with it with such violence that all I could do could not keep her so much as on the edge of it, but I found it hurried me farther and farther out from the eddy, which was on the left hand. There was no wind stirring to help me, and all that I could do with my paddles signified nothing.

However, I worked hard, till indeed my strength was almost exhausted, and kept my boat as much to the northward, that is, toward the side of the current which the eddy lay on, as I possibly could. About noon, as the sun passed the meridian, I thought I felt a little breeze of wind in my face, springing up from the SSE. This cheered my heart a little, and especially when in about half an hour more, it blew a small, gentle gale. By this time I was at a frightful distance from the island, and, had the least cloud or hazy weather intervened, I had been undone another way, too. I had no compass on board, and should never have known how to steer toward the island, if I had but once lost sight of it. But the weather continued clear, and I applied myself to get up my mast again, and spread my sail, standing away to the north as much as possible, to get out of the current. This eddy carried me about a league in my way back again directly toward the island, but about two leagues more toward the northward than the current lay, which carried me away at first, so that when I came near the island, I found myself open to the northern shore of it, that is to say, the other end of the island, opposite to that which I went out from.

When I had made something more than a league of way by the help of this current or eddy, I found that it was spent and served me no further. However, I found, that since I was to the west of the island, between the two great currents, that on the south side which had hurried me away, and that on the north, which lay about two leagues on the other side, the water was at least still, and running no way. I

had still a breeze of wind fair for me and I kept on
steering directly for the island.

About four o'clock in the afternoon, being then
within about a league of the island, I stretched across
this eddy, slanting northwest, and in about an hour
came within a mile of the shore. It being smooth
water, I soon got to land.

When I was on shore, I fell on my knees and gave
God thanks for my deliverance, resolving to lay aside
all thoughts of my deliverance by my boat. Refreshing myself with such things as I had, I brought my
boat close to the shore, in a little cove that I had
espied under some trees, and laid me down to sleep,
being quite spent with the labor and fatigue of the
voyage.

I was now at a great loss which way to get home
with my boat. I had run so much risk, and knew too
much the case to think of attempting it by the way I
went out. What might be at the other side I knew
not, nor had I any mind to run any more ventures. I
only resolved in the morning to make my way westward along the shore, and see if there was any creek
where I might lay up my frigate in safety, so as to
have her again if I wanted her. In about three miles,
or thereabouts, coasting the shore, I came to a very
good inlet, or bay, about a mile over, which narrowed
till it came to a very little rivulet, or brook, where
I found a convenient harbor for my boat, and where
she lay as if she had been in a little dock made on

purpose for her. Here I put in, and having stowed
my boat very safe, I went on shore to look about me
and see where I was.

I soon found I had but a little passed by the place
where I had been before when I traveled on foot to
that shore, so taking nothing out of my boat but my
gun and my umbrella, for it was exceedingly hot, I
began my walk. The way was comfortable enough
after such a voyage as I had been upon, and I reached
my old bower in the evening, where I found everything standing as I left it, for I always kept it in good
order, it being, as I said before, my country house.

I got over the fence, and lay down in the shade to
rest my limbs, for I was very weary. I soon fell
asleep, but judge if you can, you that read my story,
what a surprise I had, when I was awakened out of
my sleep by a voice calling me by my name several
times: "Robin, Robin, Robin Crusoe! Poor Robin
Crusoe! Where are you, Robin Crusoe? Where
are you? Where have you been?"

I was so dead asleep at first, being fatigued with
rowing, or paddling, as it is called, the first part of
the day, and walking the latter part, that I did not
awaken thoroughly. Dozing between sleeping and
waking, I thought I dreamed that somebody spoke to
me, but as the voice continued to repeat "Robin Crusoe, Robin Crusoe," at last I began to awake more
perfectly. I was at first dreadfully frightened and
started up in the utmost consternation. But no sooner

were my eyes open than I saw my Poll sitting on the top of the hedge, and immediately knew that this was he that spoke to me, for just in such bemoaning language I had used to talk to him and teach him. He had learned it so perfectly that he would sit upon my finger and lay his bill close to my face and cry, "Poor Robin Crusoe, where are you? Where have you been? How came you here?"—and such things as I had taught him.

However, even though I knew it was the parrot, and that indeed it could be nobody else, it was a good while before I could compose myself. I was amazed how the creature got thither, and that he should just keep about the place, and nowhere else, but as I was well satisfied it could be nobody but honest Poll, I got over my fright. I held out my hand and called him by his name, and the sociable creature came to me, and sat upon my thumb and continued talking to me just as if he was overjoyed to see me again. When I went home I carried him along with me.

I had had enough of rambling the sea to last me for some time. For many days I was satisfied to sit still and reflect upon the danger I had been in. I should have been very glad to have had my boat again on my side of the island, but I knew not how it was practicable to get it about. As to the east side of the island, which I had gone round, I knew well enough there was no venturing that way. My very heart would shrink, and my very blood run chill, just to think of it. As to the other side of the island, I did

not know how it might be there, but if the current
ran with the same force against the shore at the east,
as it passed by it on the other, I might run the same
risk of being driven down the stream, and carried by
the island, as I had been before of being carried away
from it. With these thoughts I contented myself to
be without any boat, though it had been the product
of so many months' labor to make it, and of so many
more to get it into the sea.

Food and Clothing ✑

I was now in the eleventh year of my residence. As I have said, my ammunition was growing low, and I set myself to study some art to trap and snare the goats, to see whether I could not catch some of them alive. I particularly wanted a she-goat great with young. To this purpose I made snares to catch them. I believe that they were more than once taken in them, but my snares were not strong, for I had no wire, and I always found them broken and my bait devoured. At length I resolved to try a pitfall. I dug several large pits in the earth, in places where I had observed that the goats used to feed, and over these pits I placed hurdles of my own making, with a great weight upon them. Several times I put barley and dry rice there without setting the trap, and I could easily perceive that the goats had gone in and eaten up the grain, for I could see the marks of their feet. At length, I set three traps in one night, and when I went the next morning, I found them all standing, and yet the bait eaten and gone. This was very discouraging. However, I altered my trap, and, not to trouble you with particulars, when I went one morning to see my traps, I found in one of them a large, old he-goat, and, in one of the others, three kids, a male and two females.

I knew not what to do with the old one. He was so fierce I dared not go into the pit to him, to bring him away alive, which was what I wanted. I could have killed him, but that was not my business, nor would it answer my end. Finally I let him out, and he ran away as if he had been frightened out of his wits. I did not then know what I afterward learned, that hunger would tame a lion. If I had let him stay there three or four days without food, and then had carried him some water to drink, and then a little grain, he would have been as tame as one of the kids, for they are very wise, tractable creatures when they are well used.

However, for the present I let him go, knowing no better at that time. Then I went to the three kids, and taking them one by one, I tied them together with strings and with some difficulty brought them all home.

It was a good while before they would feed. However, I threw them some sweet grain, and after a time it tempted them, and they began to be tame. I now found that if I expected to supply myself with goat's flesh, when I had no powder or shot left, breeding some up tame was my only way. Then perhaps I might have them about my house like a flock of sheep. But then it presently occurred to me that I must keep the tame from the wild, or else they would always run wild when they grew up. The only way to do this was to have some enclosed piece of ground, well fenced, either with hedge or pale, to keep them in so effectually that those within might not break out, or those without break in.

I first found a proper piece of ground wherein my goats might have grass and water. To enclose this pasture, I planted about it rows of a green, prickly shrub.

I was about three months hedging in the first piece, and till I had done it, I tethered the three kids in the best part of it, and made them feed as near me as possible, to make them tame. Very often I would go and carry them some barley, or a handful of rice, and feed them out of my hand, so that after my enclosure was finished, and I let them loose, they would follow me up and down, bleating after me for a handful of grain.

This answered my end, and in about a year and a half I had a flock of about twelve goats, kids and all. In two years more I had three-and-forty, besides several I took and killed for my food. After that I enclosed five different pieces of ground to feed them in, with little pens to drive them into, to take them as I wanted them, and gates out of one piece of ground into another.

But this was not all. Now I not only had goat's flesh to feed on when I pleased, but milk, too, a thing which indeed in my beginning I did not so much as think of, and which, when it came into my thoughts, was really an agreeable surprise. Now I set up my dairy, and had sometimes a gallon or two of milk in a day. And as Nature, who gives supplies of food to every creature, dictates even naturally how to make use of it, so I, that had never milked a cow, much less a goat, or seen butter or cheese made, very readily and handily, though after several trials, made both cheese and butter and never wanted for it afterward.

It would have made anyone smile to see me and my family sit down to the table which God in his mercy had furnished me here in the wilderness. I was like a king, dining alone, attended only by my servants.

Poll, as if he had been my favorite, was the only person permitted to talk to me; my dog, which was now grown old and crazy, and found no species to multiply his kind upon, sat always at my right hand; the two cats sat one on one side of the table, and one on the other, expecting now and then a bit from my hand as a mark of special favor.

These were not the two cats which I brought on shore at first, for they were both of them dead, and had been buried near my habitation by my own hands. One of them had multiplied by I know not what kind of creature, and these were two which I kept tame. The rest ran wild into the woods, and became indeed troublesome to me at last. They would often come into my house, and plunder me, too, till at last I was obliged to shoot them. After I had killed a great many, they stopped molesting me.

In this plentiful manner I lived; neither could I be said to want anything but society, and of that, some time after this, I came near having too much.

I was somewhat impatient, as I have observed, to have the use of my boat, though I was very loath to run any more risk. Therefore, sometimes I tried to contrive ways to get her about the island, and at other times I was contented enough without her. But I had a strange longing in my mind to go down to the point of the island, where, as I have said, in my last ramble, I went up the hill to see how the shore lay and how the current set, that I might see what I had to do. This inclination increased every day, and at length I resolved to travel thither by land, and following the edge of the shore, I did so.

Had anyone in England met such a man as I was, it must either have frightened them or raised a great deal of laughter. As I frequently stood still to look at myself, I could not but smile at the notion of my traveling through Yorkshire with such an equipage, and in such a dress. I had a great, high, shapeless cap, made of goat's skin, with a flap hanging down behind, as well to keep the sun from me, as to shoot the rain off from running into my neck. Nothing is so hurtful in these climates as the rain upon the flesh under the clothes. I had a short jacket of goat's skin, the skirts coming down to about the middle of my thighs, and a pair of open-kneed breeches of the same. The breeches were made of the skin of an old he-goat, whose hair hung down such a length on either side that, like pantaloons, it reached to the middle of my legs. Stockings and shoes I had none, but I made me a pair of something, I scarce know what to call them, like buskins, to flap over my legs, and lace on either side like spatterdashes,* but of a most barbarous shape, as indeed were all the rest of my clothes.

I had on a broad belt of dried goat's skin, which I drew together with two thongs of the same, instead of buckles. In a kind of frog on either side of this, instead of a sword and dagger, hung a little saw and a hatchet, one on one side, one on the other. I had another belt not so broad, and fastened in the same manner, which hung over my shoulder, and at the end of it, under my left arm, hung two pouches, both made of goat's skin, too. In one of these hung my powder, in the other my shot. At my back I carried my basket, on my shoulder my gun, and over my head a great, clumsy, ugly goat's-skin umbrella, which, after all, was the most necessary thing I had about me, next to my gun. As for my face, the color of it was really not so mulatto-like as one might expect from a man not at all careful of it, and living within nine or ten degrees of the equinox. My beard I had once allowed to grow till it was about a quarter of a yard long, but as I had both scissors and razors sufficient, I had cut it pretty short, except what grew on my upper lip, which I had trimmed into a large pair of Mahometan whiskers, such as I had seen worn by some Turks whom I saw at Sallee. Of these mustachios, or

---

* Spatterdashes are leggings or gaiters.

whiskers, I will not say they were long enough to hang my hat upon them, but they were of length and shape monstrous enough, and such as in England would have passed for frightful. But all this is by the by, for I had so few to observe my figure that it was no manner of consequence, so I will say no more about it.

I was out five or six days on my new journey. I traveled first along the seashore, directly to the place where I first brought my boat to an anchor to get up upon the rocks, and having no boat now to take care of, I went over the land a nearer way to the same height that I was upon before. When I looked out to the point of the rock which I had been obliged to double with my boat, as I said above, I was surprised to see the sea all smooth and quiet. There was no rippling, no motion, no current, any more there than in other places.

I was at a strange loss to understand this, and resolved to spend some time in observing it, to see if the sets of the tide had occasioned it. As I considered, I was presently convinced that the tide of ebb setting from the west, and joining with the current of waters from some great river on the shore, must be the occasion of this current.

This observation convinced me that I had nothing to do but to observe the ebbing and the flowing of the tide, and I might very easily bring my boat about the island again.

You are to understand that now I had, as I may call

it, two plantations in the island. One was my little fortification or tent, with the wall about it under the rock, with the cave behind me, which by this time I had enlarged into several apartments or caves, one within another.

One of these, which was the driest and largest, and had a door beyond where my wall joined to the rock, was all filled up with large earthen pots, of which I have given an account, and with fourteen or fifteen great baskets, which would hold five or six bushels each. There I laid up my stores of provision, especially my grain, some cut off short from the straw, and some rubbed out with my hands.

As for my wall, made as before, with long stakes or piles, those piles grew all like trees, and were by this time grown so big, and spread so very much, that there was not the least appearance, to anyone's view, of any habitation behind them.

Near this dwelling of mine, but a little farther within the land, and upon lower ground, lay the two pieces of ground, which I kept duly cultivated and sown, and which duly yielded me their harvest of grain in its season. Whenever I had occasion for more grain, I had more land adjoining as fit as that.

Besides this, I had my country seat, and I had now a tolerable plantation there also. First, I had my little bower, as I called it, which I kept in repair. I kept the hedge which circled it in constantly fitted up to its usual height, the ladder standing always in the inside. The trees, which at first were no more than my stakes,

but were now grown very firm and tall, I kept always
so cut, that they might spread and grow thick and
wild, and make the more agreeable shade, which they
did effectually to my mind. In the middle of this I
had my tent always standing. It was a piece of sail
spread over poles set up for that purpose and never
wanted any repair or renewing. Under this I had
made a couch, with the skins of the creatures I had
killed, and with other soft things, and a blanket laid on
them, such as belonged to our sea bedding which I
had saved, and a great watch coat to cover me. Here,
whenever I had occasion to be absent from my chief
seat, I took up my country habitation.

Adjoining to this I had my enclosures for my goats.
I had taken an inconceivable deal of pains to fence and
enclose this ground, and I was so uneasy to see it kept
entire, lest the goats should break through, that I never
stopped till with infinite labor I had stuck the outside
of the hedge so full of small stakes, so near to one
another, that it was rather a pale than a hedge. There
was scarcely room to put a hand through between
them, when those stakes grew, as they all did in the
next rainy season, and they made the enclosure
stronger than any wall.

This will testify for me that I was not idle, and that
I spared no pains to bring to pass whatever appeared
necessary for my comfortable support. I considered
that the keeping up of a breed of tame creatures would
be a living magazine of flesh, milk, butter, and cheese
for me, as long as I lived in the place, if it were to be

forty years. Keeping them in my reach depended entirely upon my perfecting my enclosures to such a degree that I might be sure of keeping them together. By this method, indeed, I succeeded so well that, when these little stakes began to grow, I found that I had planted them so very thick that I was forced to pull some of them up again.

In this place also I had my grapes growing, which I principally depended on for my winter store of raisins, and which I never failed to preserve very carefully as the best and most agreeable dainty of my whole diet. Indeed, they were not only agreeable, but wholesome, nourishing, and refreshing to the last degree.

As this was also about halfway between my other habitation and the place where I had laid up my boat, I generally stayed and lay here in my way thither, for things about her in very good order. Sometimes I I used frequently to visit my boat, and I kept all went out in her to divert myself, but no more hazardous voyages would I go, nor scarce ever above a stone's cast or two from the shore, I was so apprehensive of being hurried out of my knowledge again by the currents, or winds, or any other accident.

The Savages ♌

Now I come to a new scene of my life. It happened one day about noon as I went toward my boat that I was exceedingly surprised to see the print of a man's naked foot on the shore, which was very plain to be seen in the sand. I stood like one thunderstruck, or as if I had seen an apparition. I listened, I looked round me. I could hear nothing, see nothing. I went up to a rising ground to look farther. I went up the shore and down the shore, but it was all one, I could see no other impression but that one. I went to it again, to see if there were any more, and to observe if it might not be my fancy, but there was no room for that, for there was exactly the very print of a foot, toes, heel, and every part of a foot. How it came thither I knew not, nor could in the least imagine. I came home to my fortification, terrified to the last degree, looking behind me at every two or three steps, mistaking every bush and tree, and fancying every stump at a distance to be a man.

When I came to my castle, for so I think I called it

ever after this, I fled into it like one pursued. Whether I went over by the ladder, as first contrived, or went in at the hole in the rock, which I called a door, I cannot remember, no, nor could I remember the next morning.

I had no sleep that night. The farther I was from the occasion of my fright the greater my apprehensions were, which is something contrary to the nature of such things, and especially to the usual practice of all creatures in fear. But I was so filled with my own frightful ideas of the thing, that I formed nothing but dismal imaginations to myself, even though I was now a great way from it.

At last I concluded that it must be some of the savages of the mainland, who had wandered out to sea in their canoes, and, either driven by the currents or by contrary winds, had made the island, and had been on shore, but were going away again to sea, being as loath, perhaps, to stay in this desolate island as I would have been to have had them.

For a long time I lived in great fear, and then one day it came into my thoughts, that all this might be a mere chimera of my own, and that this foot might be the print of my own foot when I came on shore from my boat. This cheered me up a little, too, and I began to persuade myself that it was all a delusion. I considered that I could by no means tell for certain where I had trod, and where I had not.

Now I began to take courage, and to peep abroad again, for I had not stirred out of my castle for three days and nights, so that I began to starve for provision. I had little or nothing within doors but some barley cakes and water. Then I knew that my goats wanted to be milked too, which usually was my evening diversion.

Heartening myself, therefore, with the belief that this was nothing but the print of one of my own feet (and so I might be truly said to start at my own shadow), I began to go abroad again, and went to my country house to milk my flock. To see with what fear I went forward, how often I looked behind me, how I was ready, every now and then, to lay down my basket and run for my life, would have made any-one think that I was haunted with an evil conscience, or that I had been lately most terribly frightened. And so indeed I had!

However, as I went down thus two or three days, and saw nothing, I began to be a little bolder, and to think that there was really nothing in it but my own imagination. I could not persuade myself fully of this, however, till I should go down to the shore again and measure the print by my own foot. But when I came to the place first, it appeared evident to me that when I laid up my boat, I could not possibly be on shore anywhere thereabouts. Secondly, when I came to measure the mark with my own foot, I found my foot not so large by a great deal. Both these things filled my head with new imaginations.

Tortured with fear of what visiting savages might do to me, I began sorely to repent that I had dug my cave so large as to bring a door through, beyond where my fortification joined to the rock. Upon maturely considering this, therefore, I resolved to draw a second fortification, in the manner of a semicircle, at a dis-tance from my wall, just where I planted a double row of trees about twelve years before, of which I made mention. These trees had been planted so thick that when a few piles were driven between them, my wall was finished.

I had now a double wall, and my outer wall was thickened with pieces of timber, old cables, and everything I could think of to make it strong. It had in it seven holes big enough for me to put my arm through.

In the inside of this I thickened my wall to about ten feet thick, continually bringing earth out of my cave, and laying it at the foot of the wall, and walking upon it. Through the seven holes I contrived to plant muskets, which I had brought on shore out of the ship. I planted them like cannon, and fitted them into frames that held them like a carriage, so that I could fire all the seven guns in two minutes' time. This wall I was many a weary month in finishing, and I never thought myself safe till it was done.

When this was done, I stuck all the ground outside my wall, for a great way every way, full of stakes or sticks of the osier-like wood, which I found so ready to grow. I believe I must have set in nearly twenty thousand of them, leaving a pretty large space between them and my wall so that I might have room to see the enemy, and they might have no shelter from the young trees, if they attempted to approach my outer wall.

Thus in two years' time I had a thick grove, and in five or six years' time I had a wood before my dwelling, grown so monstrous thick and strong that it was indeed perfectly impassable. No man would ever have imagined that there was anything beyond it, much less a dwelling. I myself proposed to go in and out (for I left no avenue), by setting two ladders, one to a part of the rock which was low and broken in, and the other on the ledge thus formed. When the two ladders were taken down, no man living could come down to me without hurting himself, and if he did come down, he would still be on the outside of my outer wall.

Thus I took all the measures human prudence could suggest for my own preservation. It will be seen later on that they were not altogether without just reason, though I foresaw nothing at that time more than my mere fear suggested.

While I was doing this I was not altogether careless of my other affairs. I was particularly careful of my little herd of goats. They were not only a present supply to me upon every occasion, and began to be sufficient for me without the expense of powder and shot, but they also did away with the fatigue of my hunting after the wild ones. I was loath to lose the advantage of them, and to have them all to raise over again.

Accordingly, I spent some time in finding out the most retired part of the island. I finally selected three acres of choice pasture in the woods. This I now proceeded to fence and to make as firmly secure as my first meadow. Here then I placed a part of my young goats, very carefully concealed among the trees.

All this labor I was at the expense of purely from my apprehensions on the account of the print of a man's foot which I had seen. As yet, I had not seen any human creature come near the island, and I had now lived two years under these uneasinesses, which indeed made my life much less comfortable than it was before, as may well be imagined by any who know what it is to live in the constant fear of man.

One day on a trip to the end of the island, where indeed I had never been before, I was presently convinced that seeing the print of a man's foot was not such a strange thing in the island as I imagined. I began to see that it was due to a special Providence that I was cast upon the side of the island where the savages never came. If I had not been, I should easily have known that nothing was more frequent than for the canoes from the mainland, when they happened to be a little too far out at sea, to shoot over to that side of the island for harbor. I should have known, too, that as they often met and fought in their canoes, the victors, having taken any prisoners, would bring them over to this shore, where, according to their dreadful customs, being all cannibals, they would kill and eat them. More of this hereafter.

When I had come down the hill to the shore, which was, as I said above, the SW. point of the island, I was perfectly confounded and amazed, nor is it possible for me to express the horror of my mind at seeing the shore spread with skulls, hands, feet, and other bones of human bodies. Particularly, I observed a place where there had been a fire made, and a circle dug in the earth, like a cockpit, where I supposed that the savage wretches had sat down to their inhuman feastings upon the bodies of their fellow creatures. I turned away my face from the horrid spectacle, my

stomach grew sick, and I was just at the point of fainting. I could not bear to stay in the place a moment,
so I hurried up the hill again with all the speed I could,
and walked on toward my own habitation.

I observed that these wretches never came to this
island in search of what they could get. No doubt
they had often been up in the covered woody part of
it without finding anything to their purpose. I knew
that I had been here now almost eighteen years, and
had never seen the least footsteps of a human creature
there before. I might be here eighteen years more as
entirely concealed as I was now, if I did not discover
myself to them.

Yet I entertained such an abhorrence of the savage
wretches that I have been speaking of, and of the
wretched inhuman custom of their devouring and eating one another up, that I continued pensive and sad,
and kept close within my own circle for almost two
years after this. When I say my own circle, I mean
by it my three plantations, my castle, my country seat,
which I called my bower, and my enclosure in the
woods. I did not look after this for any other use
than as an enclosure for my goats, for the aversion
which Nature gave me for these hellish wretches was
such that I was as fearful of seeing them as of seeing
the Devil himself.

Time, however, and the satisfaction I had that I was
in no danger of being discovered by these people began to wear off my uneasiness about them. I began
to live just in the same composed manner as before,

only with this difference, that I used more caution and kept my eyes more about me than I did before, lest I should happen to be seen by any of them. Particularly, I was more cautious of firing my gun, lest any of them being on the island should happen to hear it. However, I was never without my gun, the two pistols, and also the old cutlass I had brought from the boat.

It was now the month of December, in my twenty-third year. The southern solstice, for winter I cannot call it, was the particular time of my harvest, and required my being pretty much abroad in the fields. One morning when I went out fairly early, even before it was thorough daylight, I was surprised to see a light of some fire upon the shore. It was at a distance from me of about two miles, toward the end of the island, where I had observed that some savages had been before. This was not on the other side, however, but to my great affliction it was on my side of the island. Climbing to the top of the hill, and pulling out my perspective glass, which I had taken on purpose, I lay down flat on my belly on the ground, and began to look for the place. I presently found that there were no less than nine naked savages sitting round a small fire they had made. They did not need it to warm them, for the weather was extremely hot, but, as I supposed, they had it to dress some of their barbarous diet of human flesh, which they had brought with them, whether alive or dead I could not know.

They had two canoes with them, which they had hauled up upon the shore. As it was then ebb tide, they seemed to me to wait for the return of the flood to go away again. It is not easy to imagine what confusion this sight put me into, especially seeing them on my side of the island, and so near me, too. However, when I observed that their coming must be always with the current of the ebb, I began to be more comfortable in my mind. I was satisfied that I might go abroad with safety all the time of the tide of flood, if they were not on shore before. When I had made this observation, I went abroad about my harvest work with more composure.

As I expected, so it proved. As soon as the tide made to the westward, I saw them all take boat, and row (or paddle as we call it) all away. I should have observed that, for an hour and more before they went off, they were dancing, and I could easily discern their postures and gestures by my glasses. I could not perceive, by my nicest observation, but that they were stark naked.

As soon as I saw them shipped and gone, I took two guns upon my shoulders and two pistols at my girdle and my great sword by my side, without a scabbard, and with all the speed that I was able to make, I went away to the hill, where I had discovered the first appearance of all. As soon as I got thither, which was not less than two hours (for I could not go swiftly, being so loaded with arms), I perceived that there had been three canoes more of savages at that place. Looking out farther, I saw that they were all at sea together making over for the mainland.

Going down to the shore, I could see the marks of horror which the dismal work they had been about had left behind it, the blood, the bones, and part of the flesh of human bodies, eaten and devoured by those wretches with merriment and sport. I was so filled with indignation at the sight, that I began now to plan the destruction of the next that I saw there, let them be who or how many soever.

It seemed evident to me that the visits which they thus made to this island were not very frequent, for it was more than fifteen months before any more of them came on shore there again, that is to say, I never saw them, or any footsteps, or signs of them in all that time. I found that they did not come in the rainy season. Yet all this while I lived uncomfortably, by reason of the constant fears I was in of their coming upon me by surprise.

While in this state of mind, I found a wonderful cave in which I might hide from the cannibals, if need be. Sometimes I went into this cave just for the comfort of seeing how well I could be concealed in it. One morning late in the last month of my twenty-third year on the island, I was going to this cave when I heard a terrible sound from the sea.

I immediately considered that this must be some ship in distress, and that they had some comrade, or some other ship in company, and fired these guns for

signals of distress and to obtain help. I had enough
presence of mind at that minute to think that though
I could not help them, it might be that they might help
me. Accordingly, I brought together all the dry
wood I could get at hand, and making a good-size
pile, I set it on fire upon the hill. The wood was dry
and blazed freely, and though the wind blew very
hard, yet it burned fairly out, so that I was certain, if
there was any such thing as a ship, they must needs
see it. No doubt they did, for as soon as my fire
blazed up, I heard another gun, and after that several

others, all from the same quarter. I plied my fire all
night long, till day broke, and when it was broad day,
and the air cleared up, I saw something at a great distance at sea, full east of the island, whether a sail, or a
hull, I could not distinguish, no, not with my glasses,
the distance was so great, and the air was still so hazy
out at sea.

I looked frequently at it all that day, and soon perceived that it did not move. I presently concluded
that it was a ship at anchor, and being eager, you may
be sure, to be satisfied, I took my gun in my hand
and ran toward the southeast side of the island, to the
rocks, where I had been formerly carried away with
the current. Getting up there, the weather by this
time being perfectly clear, I could plainly see, to my
great sorrow, the wreck of a ship cast away in the
night upon those concealed rocks which I had found
when I was out in my boat. Since they checked the
violence of the stream, and made a kind of counter-
stream, or eddy, they were the occasion of my recovering from the most desperate, hopeless condition
that ever I had been in.

I cannot explain by words what a strange longing or
hankering of desires I felt in my soul upon this sight.
Sometimes I broke out thus: "O that there had been
but one or two, nay, but one soul saved out of the ship,
to have escaped to me, that I might have had one
companion, one fellow creature, to have spoken to
me, and to have conversed with!"

In all the time of my solitary life, I never felt so

earnest, so strong a desire after the society of my fellow creatures, or so deep a regret at the want of it.

But it was not to be. Either their fate, or mine, or both, forbade it. Till the last year of my being in this island, I never knew whether any were saved out of the ship or not. I had only the affliction, some days after, of seeing the corpse of a drowned boy washed on shore, at the end of the island which was next the shipwreck. He had on a seaman's waistcoat, a pair of open-kneed linen drawers, and a blue linen shirt, but nothing to direct me to guess what nation he was of. He had nothing in his pocket but two pieces of eight and a tobacco pipe. The last was of more value to me than the first.

It was now calm, and I had a great mind to venture out in my boat to this wreck, not doubting but that I might find something on board that might be useful to me. Possibly there might be yet some living creature on board, whose life I might save. I might, by saving that life, comfort my own to the last degree. This thought clung so to my heart, that I could not be quiet, but I must venture out in my boat on board this wreck, committing the rest to God's providence. I thought that the impression was so strong upon my mind that it could not be resisted, that it must come from some invisible direction, and that I should be wanting to myself if I did not go.

Under the power of this impression, I hastened back to my castle, prepared everything for my voyage, took a quantity of bread, a great pot of fresh

water, a compass to steer by, a bottle of rum (for I
had still a great deal of that left), and a basketful of
raisins. Thus loading myself with everything necessary, I went down to my boat, which I had finally
brought around the island and hidden in a cover. I
emptied the water out of her, and got her afloat,
loaded all my cargo in her, and then went home again
for more. My second cargo was a great bagful of
rice, the umbrella to set up over my head for a shade,
another potful of fresh water, and about two dozen
of my small loaves, or barley cakes, more than before,
a bottle of goat's milk, and a cheese. All of these, with
great labor and sweat, I brought to my boat, and praying to God to direct my voyage, I put out. Rowing
or paddling the canoe along the shore, I came at last
to the utmost point of the island on that side, namely,
NE. And now I was to launch out into the ocean,
and either to venture or not to venture. I looked at
the rapid currents which ran constantly on both sides
of the island at a distance, and which were very terrible
to me, from the remembrance of the risk I had been in
before, and my heart began to fail me. I foresaw that
if I was driven into either of these currents, I should
be carried a great way out to sea, and perhaps out of
reach or sight of the island again, and that then, since
my boat was so small, if any little gale of wind should
rise, I should be inevitably lost.

These thoughts so oppressed me that I began to consider giving up the enterprise. I steered my boat into
a creek and stepped out. Securing my boat, I hastened

to climb a little hill which sufficiently overlooked the
sea both ways. Here I found that as the current of
the ebb set out close by the south point of the island,
so the current of the flood set in close by the shore of
the north side. Therefore I had nothing to do but to
keep to the north side of the island on my return, and
I should do well enough. Encouraged by this observation, I resolved to set out with the first of the tide
the next morning. I reposed myself for the night in
my canoe, under the watch coat I mentioned.

Early the next morning I launched out. I first made
a little out to sea, full north, till I began to feel the
benefit of the current, which set eastward, and which
carried me at a great rate. Having a strong steerage
with my paddle, I went at high speed directly for the
wreck, and in less than two hours I came up to it.

It was a dismal sight to look at. The ship, which by
its building was Spanish, stuck fast, jammed in between
two rocks. All the stern and quarter of her were
beaten to pieces by the sea, and as her forecastle, which
stuck on the rocks, had run on with great violence, her
mainmast and foremast were brought by the board,
that is to say, broken short off, but her bowsprit was
sound, and the head and bow appeared firm. When I
came close to her, a dog appeared upon her, who, seeing me coming, yelped and cried. As soon as I called
him, he jumped into the sea to come to me. I took
him into the boat, and found him almost dead for
hunger and thirst. I gave him a cake of my bread,
and he ate it like a ravenous wolf that had been starv-

ing for a fortnight in the snow. I then gave the poor creature some fresh water, with which, if I would have let him, he would have burst himself.

After this I went on board. The first sight I met with was two men drowned in the cookroom, or forecastle of the ship, with their arms fast about one another. I concluded, as is indeed probable, that when the ship struck, it being in a storm, the sea broke so high, and so continually over her, that the men were not able to bear it, and were strangled with the constant rushing in of the water, as much as if they had been under water. Besides the dog, there was nothing left in the ship that had life, or any goods that I could see, but what were spoiled by the water. There were some casks of liquor, whether wine or brandy I knew not, which lay lower in the hold, and which, the water being ebbed out, I could see, but they were too big to meddle with. I saw several chests, which I believed belonged to some of the seamen, and I got two of them into the boat, without examining what was in them.

Had the stern of the ship been whole and the fore part broken off, I am persuaded that I might have made a good voyage, for, by what I found in these two chests, I had reason to suppose that the ship had had a great deal of wealth on board. If I may guess by the course she steered, she must have been bound from Buenos Aires or the Rio de la Plata, in the south part of America, beyond the Brazils, to Havana, in the Gulf of Mexico, and so perhaps to Spain.

I found besides these chests a little cask full of liq-

uor, of about twenty gallons, which I got into my
boat with much difficulty. There were several muskets in the cabin and a great powder horn, with about
four pounds of powder in it. I had no need for the
muskets, so I left them, but I took the powder horn.
I took a fire shovel and tongs which I wanted extremely; also two little brass kettles, a copper pot to
make chocolate, and a gridiron. With this cargo and
the dog I came away, the tide beginning to make home
again. The same evening, about an hour before night,
I reached the island again, wearied and fatigued to the
last degree.

I reposed that night in the boat, and in the morning
I resolved to harbor what I had gotten in my new
cave, not to carry it home to my castle. After refreshing myself, I got all my cargo on shore, and began to
examine it. When I came to open the chests, I found
several things I wanted; for example, I found in one a
fine case of bottles, of an extraordinary kind, and filled
with cordial waters, fine, and very good. The bottles
held about three pints each, and were tipped with
silver. I found two pots of very good succades, or
sweetmeats, so fastened on top that the salt water had
not hurt them, and two more of the same, which the
water had spoiled. I found some very good shirts,
which were very welcome to me, and about a dozen
and a half of white linen handkerchiefs, and colored
neckcloths. The handkerchiefs were also very welcome, being exceedingly refreshing to wipe my face
on in a hot, dry day. Besides this, when I came to the

till in the chest, I found there three great bags of pieces of eight, which held about eleven hundred pieces in all. In one of them, wrapped up in a paper, there were six doubloons of gold, and some small bars of gold; I suppose they might all weigh nearly a pound.

The other chest I found had some clothes in it, but of little value. By the circumstances it must have belonged to the gunner's mate, though there was no powder in it, but about two pounds of glazed powder in three small flasks, kept, I suppose, for charging their fowling pieces on occasion. Upon the whole, I got very little by this voyage that was of much use to me, for, as for the money, I had no manner of occasion for it. It was to me as the dirt under my feet, and I would have given it all for three or four pairs of English shoes and stockings and a good coat.

Friday ᴄ

Oɴᴇ night, in the rainy season, in March, the four-and-twentieth year of my first setting foot in this land of solitariness, I had the following dream. I thought that as I was going out in the morning, as usual, from my castle, I saw upon the shore two canoes, and eleven savages coming to land. They were bringing with them another savage, whom they were going to kill, in order to eat him. Suddenly the savage that they were going to kill made his escape and ran for his life. Then I thought in my dream that he came running into my little grove, before my fortification, to hide himself. I, seeing him and not perceiving that the others sought him that way, showed myself to him and encouraged him. He knelt down to me, seeming to pray to me to assist him, upon which I showed him my ladder, made him go up, and helped him into my cave, and he became my servant. I thought that as soon as I had got this man, I said to myself, "Now I may venture to the mainland, for this fellow will serve me as a pilot and tell me what to do,

and whither to go for provisions, and whither not to
go for fear of being devoured; what places to venture
into, and what to escape."

I awoke with this thought, and was under such
inexpressible impressions of joy at the prospect of my
escape in my dream, that the disappointment I felt
upon coming to myself and finding that it was no more
than a dream was really extravagant the other way, and
threw me into a very great dejection of spirits. Upon
this, however, I made this conclusion, that my only
way to go about an attempt for an escape was to try
to get a savage in my possession.

About a year and a half after my dream I was surprised one morning early to see no less than five canoes
all on shore together, on my side of the island, and the
people who belonged to them all landed. The number of them broke all my measures, for I could not tell
what to think of it, or how to take my measures to
attack twenty or thirty men singlehanded, so I lay still
in my castle, perplexed and discomforted. However,
I put myself into the position for an attack that I had
formerly planned, and was ready for action, if anything happened. I waited a good while, listening to
hear if they made any noise. At length, being very
impatient, I set my guns at the foot of my ladder, and
clambered up to the top of the hill by my two stages,
as usual. I was careful to stand, however, so that my
head did not appear above the hill, so that they could
not perceive me by any means. I here observed, by
the help of my perspective glass, that they were no less

than thirty in number, that they had a fire kindled, and
that they had meat dressed. How they cooked it, that
I knew not, or what it was, but they were all dancing
round the fire.

While I was thus looking at them, I perceived, by
my perspective glass, two miserable wretches dragged
from the boats, where, it seems, they were laid by, and
were now brought out for the slaughter. I perceived
one of them immediately fall, being knocked down, I
suppose, with a club, or wooden sword, for that was
their way. Two or three others went to work cutting

him open for their cookery, while the other victim was left standing by himself till they should be ready for him. In that very moment the poor wretch, seeing himself a little at liberty, was inspired with hopes of life. He started away from them, and ran with incredible swiftness along the sands, directly toward that part of the coast where I was.

I was dreadfully frightened (that I must acknowledge) when I saw him run my way, and especially when, as I thought, I saw him pursued by the whole body. I expected that part of my dream would come to pass, and that he would take shelter in my grove. I could not depend, by any means, upon my dream for the rest of it, that the savages would not pursue him thither, and find him there. However, I kept my station, and my spirits began to recover when I found that there were not more than three men that followed him. Still more was I encouraged, when I found that he outstripped them exceedingly in running, and gained ground on them, so that if he could but hold out for about half an hour, he would fairly get away from them all.

There was between them and my castle the creek, which I knew the poor wretch much necessarily swim over, or he would be taken there. However, when the savage who was escaping came thither, he made nothing of it, though the tide was then up, but plunging in, he swam through it in about thirty strokes, or thereabouts, landed, and ran on with exceeding strength and swiftness. When the three pursuers came to the creek, I found that two of them could swim, but the third could not, and that he, standing on the other side, looked at the others, but went no farther, and soon after went quietly back again, which, as it happened, was very well for him.

I observed that the two who swam were twice as long swimming over the creek as the fellow was that fled from them. It came now very warmly upon my thoughts, and indeed irresistibly, that now was my time to get a servant, and perhaps, a companion or assistant, and that I was called plainly by Providence to save this poor creature's life. I immediately got down the ladders, caught up my two guns, for they were both at the foot of the ladders, and getting up again with the same haste to the top of the hill, I crossed toward the sea. I had a very shortcut, all downhill, and I soon clapped myself in the way between the pursuers and the pursued, hallooing aloud to him that fled. He, looking back, was at first as much frightened at me as at them, but I beckoned with my hand to him to come back. In the meantime I slowly advanced toward the two that followed, then rushing at once upon the foremost, I knocked him down with the stock of my piece. I was loath to fire, because I did not want the rest to hear, although at that distance it would not have been easily heard. They were out of sight of the smoke, too, and would not have known what to make of it. When I knocked this fellow down, the other who followed him stopped, as if he had been frightened, and I advanced a pace toward him. As I came nearer, I perceived presently that he had a bow and arrow, and was fitting it to shoot at me, so I was then necessitated to shoot at him first, which I did, and killed him at the first shot.

The poor savage who fled, but had stopped, though he saw both his enemies fallen, and killed (as he thought), yet was so frightened with the noise and fire of my piece, that he stood stockstill, and neither came forward nor went backward, though he seemed rather more inclined to fly still, than to come on. I hallooed again to him, and made signs to him to come forward, which he easily understood, and came a little way, then stopped again, and then a little farther, and stopped again. Then he stood trembling, as if he had been taken prisoner, and was just about to be killed, as his two enemies were. I beckoned to him again to come to me, and gave him all the signs of encouragement that I could think of. He came nearer and nearer, kneeling down every ten or twelve steps, in token of acknowledgment for saving his life. I smiled at him, and looked pleasantly, and beckoned to him to come still nearer. At length he came close to me, and then he knelt down again, kissed the ground, and, taking my foot, set it upon his head. This, it seems, was his way of swearing to be my slave forever. I took him up, and made much of him, and encouraged him all I could.

I perceived that the savage whom I had knocked down was not killed, but only stunned with the blow, and was beginning to come to himself. So I pointed

to him, showing the savage that he was not dead. Upon this he spoke some words to me, and though I could not understand them, yet I thought they were pleasant to hear, for they were the first sound of a man's voice that I had heard, my own excepted, for more than five-and-twenty years. But there was no time for such reflections now. The savage who was knocked down recovered himself so far as to sit upon the ground, and I perceived that the savage with me began to be afraid. When I saw that, I pointed my

other gun at the man, as if I would shoot him. At this
my savage, for so I call him now, made a motion to me
to lend him my sword, which hung naked in a belt
by my side.

He no sooner had it than he ran to his enemy and at
one blow cleverly cut off his head. No executioner in
Germany could have done it sooner or better. I
thought this very strange for one who, I had reason to
believe, had never seen a sword in his life before, except the wooden swords his people used. However,
it seems, as I learned afterward, that they make their
wooden swords so sharp, so heavy, and the wood is so
hard, that they could cut off heads and arms with
them, and at one blow, too. When he had done this,
he came laughing to me in sign of triumph, and
brought me the sword again, and then laid it down,
with the head of the savage he had killed, just before
me.

He was astonished how I had killed the other man
so far off, and going to him, he stood like one amazed,
looking at him, turning him, first on one side, then on
the other. He looked at the wound the bullet had
made, which was in the breast, where it had made a
hole, and no great quantity of blood had followed,
but he had bled inwardly, for he was quite dead.
Then he took his bows and arrows, and came back,
and I motioned for us to go away, making signs that
more might come after them. Upon this, he signed to
me, that he should bury them with sand, that they
might not be seen by the rest, if they followed. I

made signs for him to do so and he fell to work, and
had them buried in the sand in about a quarter of an
hour.

I then called him away, and took him not to my
castle, but my cave, on the farther part of the island.
So I did not let my dream come to pass in that respect,
namely, that he came into my grove for shelter. Here
I gave him bread and a bunch of raisins to eat, and a
draft of water, which he was in great distress for, because of his running. When I had refreshed him, I
made signs for him to go to sleep, pointing to a place
where I had laid a great parcel of rice straw, and a
blanket upon it, which I used to sleep upon myself
sometimes. The poor creature lay down and went to
sleep.

He was a handsome fellow, perfectly well made,
tall and well-shaped, and, as I thought, about twenty-
six years of age. He had a very good countenance,
not a fierce and surly aspect, but he seemed to have
something very manly in his face, and he had all the
sweetness and softness of a European in his countenance, too, especially when he smiled. His hair was
long and black, not curled like wool, his forehead very
high and large, and there was a great vivacity and
sparkling sharpness in his eyes. The color of his skin
was not quite black, but very tawny, and yet not of
an ugly, yellow, nauseous tawny, but of a bright kind
of dun olive color that had in it something very agreeable, though not very easy to describe. His face was
round and plump, his nose small, not flat like those of

the Negroes, his mouth was very good, with thin lips, and his teeth fine, well set, and white as ivory.

After he had slumbered about half an hour, he waked, and came out of the cave to me, for I had been milking the goats in the enclosure just by. When he saw me, he came running, and laid himself on the ground again, with all the possible sings of a humble, thankful disposition, making many gestures to show it. At last he laid his head flat upon the ground, close to my foot, and set my other foot upon his head, as he had done before, and after this, made all the signs to me of subjection, servitude, and submission imaginable, to let me know how much he would serve me as long as he lived. I understood him in many things, and let him know I was well pleased with him. In a little time I began to speak to him, and teach him to speak to me. First I made him know that his name should be Friday, which was the day I saved his life. I likewise taught him to say, "Master," and then let him know that that was to be my name. I also taught him to say, "Yes," and "No," and to know the meaning of them. I gave him some milk in an earthen pot, and some bread, and let him see me drink some before him, and sop my bread in it, which he quickly imitated, and made signs that it was very good.

I kept there with him all that night, but as soon as it was day, I took him away with me. As we went by the place where he had buried the two men, he pointed exactly to the spot, and showed me the marks he had made to find them again. I then led him to the top of the hill, to see if his enemies were gone, and pulling out my glass, I looked, and saw plainly the place where they had been, but no appearance of them or their canoes. Evidently they were quite gone.

When we had done this, we came back to our castle, where I gave Friday first of all a pair of linen drawers, which I had out of the poor gunner's chest I found in the wreck, and which, with a little alteration, fitted him very well. Then I made him a jacket of goat's skin, as well as I was able, and I gave him a cap, which I had made of a hare's skin. Thus he was dressed, for the present, tolerably well, and mighty well was he pleased to see himself almost as well clothed as his master. He went awkwardly in these things at first. Wearing the drawers was very awkward to him, and the sleeves of the jacket rubbed his shoulders and the inside of his arms, but he soon got used to them.

The next day after I came home to my hut with him, I began to consider where I should lodge him. I made a little tent for him in the vacant place between the two fortifications, in the inside of the last, and in the outside of the first. As there was an entrance there into my cave, I made a formal framed doorcase, and a door to it of boards, and set it up in the passage, a little within the entrance, and causing the door to open in the inside, I barred it up in the night, taking in my ladders, too. So Friday could no way come at me in the inside of my innermost wall, without making so much noise in getting over, that it must needs awaken me, for my first wall had now a complete roof over it of long poles, covering all my tent, and leaning up to the side of the hill. The poles were laid across with small sticks instead of laths, and then thatched over thickly with the rice straw, which was as strong as reeds. At the hole or place which was left to go in or out by the ladder, I had placed a kind of trapdoor, which, if it had been attempted on the outside, would not have opened at all, but would have fallen down and made a great noise. I took care to take all the weapons in with me and lay them by my side every night.

But I needed none of these precautions, for never was a more faithful, loving, sincere servant than Friday was to me. He was without passions, sullenness, or designs; his very affections were tied to me, like those of a child to its father, and, I dare say, he would have sacrificed his life for the saving of my own, upon any occasion whatever.

I was greatly delighted with him, and made it my business to teach him everything that was proper and useful, and especially to make him speak, and understand me when I spoke. He was a very apt scholar, and he was so merry, so diligent, and so pleased when he could understand me, or make me understand him, that it was very pleasant for me to talk to him. And now my life began to be very easy and happy.

After I had been two or three days in my castle, I thought that in order to get Friday away from this horrid way of feeding, and from the relish of a canni-

bal's stomach, I ought to let him taste other flesh. So
I took him out with me one morning to the woods. I
saw a she-goat lying down in the shade, and two young
kids close by her. At once I caught hold of Friday.
"Stop," said I; "stand still," and made signs to him
not to stir. Immediately I raised my gun, shot, and
killed one of the kids. The poor creature who had, at
a distance indeed, seen me kill the savage, his enemy,
but did not know, and could not imagine how it was
done, was greatly surprised. He trembled, and shook,
and looked so amazed, that I thought he would sink
down. He ripped up his waistcoat to feel if he was
not wounded. As I found, he thought that I was resolved to kill him, for he came and knelt down to me,
and, embracing my knees, said a great many things
that I did not understand, but I could see that his meaning was to pray to me not to kill him.

I soon found a way to convince him that I would
do him no harm. Taking him up by the hand, I
laughed at him, and, pointing to the kid I had killed,
beckoned to him to run and get it, which he did.

I brought home the kid, and the same evening took
the skin off, and cut it up as well as I could. Having
a pot for that purpose, I boiled or stewed some of the
flesh, and made some very good broth. After I had
begun to eat some, I gave some to my man, who
seemed very glad of it, and liked it very well. It was
very strange to him, however, to see me eat salt with it.
He made a sign to me that the salt was not good to eat,
and putting a little into his own mouth, he seemed to

nauseate at it, and would spit and sputter, washing his mouth with fresh water after it. On the other hand, I took some meat in my mouth without salt, and I pretended to spit and sputter for want of salt, as fast as he had done at it, but it would not do.

Having thus fed him with boiled meat and broth, I was resolved to feast him the next day with roasting a piece of the kid. This I did by hanging it before the fire on a string, as I had seen many people do in England, setting two poles up, one on each side of the fire, and one across the top, and tying the string to the cross stick, letting the meat turn continually. This Friday admired very much. When he came to taste the flesh, he took so many ways to tell me how well he liked it, that I could not but understand him. At last he told me he would never eat man's flesh any more, which I was very glad to hear.

The next day I set him to work beating some corn out, and sifting it in the manner I used to do. He soon understood how to do it as well as I, especially after he had seen what the meaning of it was, and that it was to make bread of. After that I let him see me make my bread, and bake it too; and in a little time Friday was able to do all the work for me as well as I could do it myself.

I began now to consider that having two mouths to feed instead of one, I must provide more ground for my harvest, and plant a larger quantity of corn than I used to do. Accordingly, I marked out a larger piece of land, and began the fence in the same manner as before. Friday not only worked very hard, but very cheerfully. I told him that it was for corn to make more bread, because he was now with me, and that I might have enough for him and myself, too. He appeared to understand that part, and let me know that he would work the harder for me, if I would tell him what to do.

This was the pleasantest year of all the life I led in this place. Friday began to talk pretty well, and chatted a great deal to me. He understood the names of almost everything I had occasion to call for, and of every place I had occasion to send him to, so that I began to have some use of my tongue again. Besides the pleasure of talking to him, I had a singular satisfaction in the fellow himself. His simple, unfeigned honesty appeared to be more and more every day, and I began really to love the creature, and I believe he loved me as much as possible.

I had a mind once to see if he had any lingering inclination for his own country. I had taught him English so well that he could answer almost any questions, so I asked him whether the nation that he belonged to never conquered in battle. At this he smiled, and said, "Yes, yes; we always fight the better," and so we began the following discourse:

"You always fight the better!" said I. "How came you to be taken prisoner, then, Friday?"

Friday. My nation beat much for all that.

Master. How beat? If your nation beat them, how came you to be taken?

Friday. They more than my nation in the place where me was: they take one, two, three, and me. My nation beat them in yonder place, where me no was; there my nation take one, two, great thousand.

Master. But why did not your side recover you from the hands of your enemies, then?

Friday. They run one, two, three, and me, and make go in the canoe. My nation have no canoe that time.

Master. Well, Friday, and what does your nation do with the men they take? Do they carry them away, and eat them, as these did?

Friday. Yes, my nation eat mans too, eat all up.

Master. Where do they carry them?

Friday. Go to other place, where they think.

Master. Do they come hither?

Friday. Yes, yes, they come hither: come other else place.

Master. Have you been here with them?

Friday. Yes, I been here. (Points to the NW. side of the island, which it seems was their side.)

By this I understood that my man Friday had formerly been among the savages who had come on shore on the farther parts of the island, on maneating occasions such as he had been brought for. Some time after, when I took courage to carry him to that side, he knew the place, and told me that he had been there once when they had eaten up twenty men, two women, and one child.

After I had had this discourse with him, I asked him how far it was from our island to the shore and whether the canoes were not often lost. He told me that there was no danger, no canoes ever lost, but that, after a little way out to sea, there was a current, and the wind was always one way in the morning, and the other in the afternoon.

This I thought to be no more than the sets of the tide, going out or coming in, but I afterward understood that it was caused by the great draft and reflux of the mighty river Oronoque. In the mouth of this river, as I thought afterward, our island lay. I thought that this land, which I perceived to the W. and NW., was the great island Trinidad, on the north point of the mouth of the river. I asked Friday a thousand questions about the country, the inhabitants, the sea, the coast, and what nations were near. He told me all he knew, with the greatest openness imaginable. I asked him the names of the several nations of his sort of people, but could get no other names than Caribs. From this I easily understood that these were the Caribbes, which our maps place on that part of America which reaches from the mouth of the river Oronoque to Guiana, and onward to St. Martha. He told me that up a great way beyond the moon, by which he meant the region west of their country, there dwelt white, bearded men like me, and pointed to my great whiskers, which I mentioned before, and that they had killed "much mans." By all this I un-

derstood that he meant the Spaniards, whose cruelties
in America had been spread over whole countries,
and were remembered by all the nations from father
to son.

I inquired if he could tell me how I might come
from this island, and get among those white men. He
told me yes, yes, I might go in "two canoe." I could
not understand what he meant by "two canoe," till at
last, with great difficulty, I found that he meant that it
must be a large boat, as big as two canoes.

This part of Friday's discourse began to interest me
very much. From this time I entertained some hopes
that, one time or other, I might find an opportunity to
make my escape from this place, and that this poor
savage might be a means of helping me to do it.

I now wanted to lay a foundation of religious
knowledge in Friday's mind, so I asked him one time
who made him. The poor creature did not understand me, but thought I had asked him who his father
was. But I took it another way, and asked him who
made the sea, the ground he walked on, and the hills
and the woods. He told me that it was one old Benamuckee, that lived beyond all. He could describe
nothing of this great person, but that he was very old,
much older, he said, than the sea or the land, than the
moon or the stars. I asked him then, if this person had
made all things, why all things did not worship him.
He looked very grave, and with a perfect look of in-
nocence said, "All things said O to him." I asked him

if the people who died in his country went away anywhere. He said, that they all went to Benamuckee.
Then I asked him whether those they ate up went
thither too. He said, "Yes."

From these things I began to instruct him in the
knowledge of the true God. I told him that the great
Maker of all things lived up there, pointing up toward
heaven; that He governed the world by the same
power and providence by which He had made it; that
He was omnipotent, could do everything for us, give
everything to us, take everything from us. Thus, by
degrees, I opened his eyes. He listened with great attention, and received with pleasure the notion of Jesus
Christ's being sent to redeem us, and of the manner of
making our prayers to God, and His being able to hear
us, even in heaven.

I sent Friday for something a great way off, and
while he was gone I prayed to God that He would en-
able me to instruct this poor savage.

I had, God knows, more sincerity than knowledge,
in all the methods I took for this poor creature's in-
struction. I must acknowledge what I believe all that
act upon the same principle will find, that, in laying
things open to him, I really informed and instructed
myself in many things that I either did not know or
had not fully considered before, but which occurred
naturally to my mind, upon my searching into them
for the information of this poor savage. I had more
pleasure in my inquiry after things upon this occasion

than ever I had felt before, so that whether this poor wild wretch was the better for me or not, I had great reason to be thankful that he had come to me.

After Friday and I became more intimately acquainted, and he could understand almost all that I said to him, and could speak fluently, though in broken English to me, I told him my story. I let him into the mystery of gunpowder and bullets, and taught him how to shoot. I gave him a knife, which he was wonderfully delighted with, and I made him a belt with a frog hanging to it, such as in England we wear

hangers* in, and in the frog, instead of a hanger, I gave
him a hatchet.

I described to him the countries of Europe, and
particularly England, which I came from. I told him
how we lived, how we worshiped God, how we be-
haved to one another, and how we traded in ships to all
parts of the world. I gave him an account of the
wrecked vessel which I had been on board of, and
showed him, as nearly as I could, the place where she
had lain. She had been gone for some time.

I showed him the ruins of our boat, which we lost
when I escaped, and which was now fallen almost to
pieces. Upon seeing this boat, Friday stood musing
some time, and said nothing. I asked him what he
studied upon. At last he said, "Me see such boat like
come to place at my nation."

I did not understand him for a great while, but at
last, when I had examined farther into it, I understood
by him, that a boat, such as that had been, came on
shore upon the country where he lived, that is, as he
explained it, was driven thither by stress of weather.
I presently imagined that some European ship must
have been cast away upon their coast and the boat must
have gotten loose, and been driven ashore. I was so
dull that I never once thought of men making their
escape from a wreck thither, so I only inquired for a
description of the boat.

Friday described the boat to me well enough, but
he brought me better to understand him when he

---

* A hanger is a short, usually curved sword.

added, with some warmth, "We save the white mans from drown."

Then I asked him if there were any white mans, as he called them, in the boat.

"Yes," he said, "the boat full of white mans."

I asked, "How many?"

He told me upon his fingers seventeen.

I asked, "What became of them?"

He told me, "they live, they dwell at my nation."

This put new thoughts into my head again, for I presently imagined that these might be the men belonging to the ship that was cast away in sight of my island, who, after the ship was stuck on the rock, and they saw her inevitably lost, had saved themselves in their boat, and were landed upon that wild shore among savages.

Upon this I inquired of him more critically what had become of them. He assured me that they still lived there and had been there about four years. He said that the savages let them alone and gave them food. I asked him how it came to pass that they did not kill them and eat them. He said, "No, they make brother with them," meaning, as I understood him, that they had made a truce. Then he added, "They no eat mans, but when make the war fight." That is to say, they never eat any men, but such as come to fight with them, and are taken in battle.

It was after this, some considerable time, that we were on the top of the hill, at the east side of the island, from whence I had, in a clear day, discovered the mainland, or continent of America. The weather was very clear, and as Friday looked very earnestly toward the mainland, he began jumping and dancing, and called out to me. I asked him what was the matter.

"O joy!" says he. "O glad! There see my country! There my nation!"

I observed an extraordinary sense of pleasure appear in his face, his eyes sparkled and his countenance was alight with strange eagerness, as if he wanted to be in his own country again. This observation of mine put a great many thoughts into me, which made me at first not so easy about my new man Friday as I had been before. I did not doubt, that if Friday could get back to his own nation again, he would not only forget all his religion, but all his obligations to me.

But I wronged the poor honest creature very much, for which I was very sorry afterward. However, as my jealousy increased and held me some weeks, I was a little more circumspect, and not so familiar and kind to him as before, in which I was certainly in the wrong.

While my jealousy of him lasted, I was every day pumping him, to see if he would disclose any of the new thoughts which I suspected were in him, but I found everything he said so honest and so innocent, that I could find nothing to nourish my suspicion. In spite of all my uneasiness, he made me at last entirely his own again, nor did he in the least perceive that I was uneasy, and therefore I could not suspect him of deceit.

One day we were walking up the same hill. The weather this time was hazy at sea, so that we could not see the continent. "Friday," I said, "do not you wish yourself in your own country, your own nation?"

"Yes," he said; "I be much glad to be at my own nation."

"What would you do there?" I asked. "Would you turn wild again, eat man's flesh again, and be savage as you were before?"

Friday shook his head and said, "No, no; Friday tell them to live good, tell them to pray God, tell them to eat corn bread, cattle flesh, milk; no eat man again."

"Why, then," I told him, "they will kill you."

Seeing my alarm, he looked grave and said, "No, they no kill me; they willing love learn." He meant by this that they would be willing to learn. He added that they had learned much of the bearded men that had come in the boat. Then I asked if he would go back to his people. He smiled at that, and told me he could not swim so far. I told him I would make a canoe for him. He told me he would go, if I would go with him.

"I go!" said I. "Why they will eat me if I come there!"

"No, no," said he, "me make them no eat you; me make they much love you." He meant he would tell them how I had killed his enemies, and saved his life, and so he would make them much love me.

From this time, I confess, I had a mind to venture over, and see if I could possibly join with these bearded men, who, I made no doubt, were Spaniards or Portuguese. I did not doubt that, if I could, we might find some method to escape from thence, being upon the continent, and a good company together, better than I could from an island, forty miles off the shore, and alone without help. So, after some days I took Friday to work again, and told him that I would give him a boat to go back to his own nation. Accordingly I took him to my frigate. When I had cleared it of the water, I brought it out, showed it to him, and we both went into it.

I found that he was very dexterous at managing it, and would make it go almost as swiftly again as I could, so I said to him, "Well, now, Friday, shall we go to your nation?" He looked very dull at my saying so, which, it seems, was because he thought the boat was too small to go so far. I told him then I had a bigger, so the very next day I went to the place where the first boat lay, which I had made, but which I could not get into the water. He said that that was big enough, but as I had taken no care of it, and it had lain two- or three-and-twenty years there, the sun had split and dried it so that it was in a manner rotten. Friday told me that such a boat would do very well and would carry "much enough vittle, drink, bread."

Upon the whole, I was by this time so fixed upon my design of going over with him to the continent, that I told him that we would go and make one as big as that, and he should go home in it. He answered not one word, but looked very grave and sad. I asked him what was the matter with him.

He answered with a question. "Why you angry mad with Friday? What me done?"

I asked him what he meant, and told him that I was not angry with him at all.

"No angry! No angry!" said he, repeating the words several times. "Why send Friday home away to my nation?"

"Why," said I, "Friday, did you not say you wished you were there?"

"Yes, yes," said he, "wish we both there; no wish Friday there, no master there." In a word, he would not think of going there without me.

"You shall go without me; leave me here to live by myself as I did before."

He looked confused at this, running to one of the hatchets which he used to wear, he took it up hastily, and gave it to me.

"What must I do with this?" said I to him.

"You take kill Friday," said he.

"What must I kill you for?" said I again.

He returned very quickly, "What you send Friday away for? Take kill Friday; no send Friday away."

As he spoke, tears stood in his eyes, and I was so

affected that I said that I would never send him away,
if he was willing to stay with me.

I found that all the foundation of his desire to go
to his own country was laid in his ardent affection to
the people, and his hopes of my doing them good.
This was a thing which I had no notion of myself, so
I had not the least thought, or intention, or desire of
undertaking it. But still I had a strong inclination to
attempt an escape, founded on the supposition gathered from the former discourse, that there were seventeen bearded men there. Therefore, without any
more delay, I went to work with Friday, to find out
a great tree proper to fell, and make a large canoe,
for the voyage. After searching some time, Friday
at last pitched upon a tree, for I found he knew much
better than I what kind of wood was fittest for it. I
cannot tell, to this day, what wood to call the tree we
cut down, except that it was very like the tree we call
fustic,* or between that and the Nicaragua wood, for
it was much of the same color and smell. Friday was
for burning the hollow or cavity of this tree out, to
make it into a boat, but I showed him how to cut it
out with tools. After I had showed him he did it very
handily, and after about a month's hard labor we finished it, and made it very handsome, especially when
with our axes, which I showed him how to handle,
we cut and hewed the outside into the true shape of

---

* The fustic is a large tree in South America. Its wood, which is soft, is
used as a yellow dye.

a boat. After this, however, it cost us nearly a fortnight's time to get her along, as it were, inch by inch,
upon great rollers, into the water. When she was in,
she would have carried twenty men with us.

It amazed me to see with what dexterity and how
swiftly my man Friday would manage her, turn her,
and paddle her along. So I asked him if he would,
and if we might venture over in her.

"Yes," he said, "me venture over in her very well,
though great wind blow."

However, I had a further design that he knew nothing of, and that was to make a mast and a sail, and to
fit her with an anchor and a cable. As to the mast,
that was easy enough to get. I pitched upon a straight
young cedar tree, which I found near the place, and
of which there were plenty in the island. I set Friday
to work to cut it down, and gave him directions how
to shape and order it, but the sail was my particular
care. I knew I had pieces of old sails, but as I had
had them now twenty-six years by me, and had not
been very careful to preserve them, they were nearly
all rotten. However, I found two pieces which appeared pretty good, and with a great deal of pains and
awkward, tedious stitching, for want of needles, I at
length made a three-cornered ugly thing, such as we
call in England a shoulder-of-mutton sail. It was to
go with a boom at the bottom, and a little short sprit
at the top, such as usually our ships' longboats sail
with, and such as I best knew how to manage, because

it was such a one as I used in the boat in which I made my escape from Barbary.

I was nearly two months rigging and fitting out my mast and sails, for I fitted them very completely, making a small stay, and a sail, or foresail to it, to assist, if we should turn to windward. What was more than all, I fixed a rudder to the stern of her to steer with, and though I was but a bungling shipwright, yet, as I knew the usefulness and even necessity of such a thing, I applied myself with so much pains to do it, that at last I brought it to pass.

After all this was done, I had my man Friday to teach as to what belonged to the navigation of my boat. He knew very well how to paddle the canoe, but he knew nothing about a sail and a rudder, and how the sail gibed, and filled this way or that way, as the course we sailed changed. When he saw this, he stood like one astonished and amazed. However, with a little use, I made all these things familiar to him, and he became an expert sailor, except that I could make him understand very little of the compass. However, there was not much occasion for the compass in these parts.

I was now entered on the seven-and-twentieth year of my captivity in this place. The three last years when I had Friday with me ought to be left out of the account, for my life was quite another kind than in all the rest of the time. I kept the anniversary of my landing here with the same thankfulness to God

for His mercies as at first. If I had had such cause
of acknowledgment at first, I had much more so now,
having such additional testimonies of the care of Providence over me, and the great hopes I had of being
effectually and speedily delivered. I had a persistent
impression that my deliverance was at hand, and that
I should not be another year in this place. However,
I went on with all my work as usual.

The rainy season was in the meantime upon me,
when I kept more within doors than at other times.
We had stowed our new vessel as securely as we could,
bringing her up into the creek, where, as I said in the
beginning, I landed my rafts from the ship. Thus we
waited for the months of November and December,
in which I planned to make my venture.

The Savages Return ❧

WHEN the settled season began to come in, the first thing I did was to lay by a certain quantity of provisions as the store for our voyage. I intended in a week or a fortnight's time to open the dock and launch out our boat. I was busy one morning upon something of this kind, when I called to Friday and bade him go to the seashore and see if he could find a turtle or a tortoise—a thing which we generally got once a week for the sake of the eggs, as well as the flesh. Friday had not been long gone, when he came running back, and fairly flew over my outer wall, or fence. Before I had time to speak to him, he cried out to me, "O master! O master! O sorrow! O bad!"

"What's the matter, Friday?" said I.

"Oh, yonder there," said he, "one, two, three canoe! One, two, three!"

By this way of speaking, I concluded that there were six; but, on inquiry, I found that there were but three.

"Well, Friday," said I, "do not be frightened," and I heartened him up as well as I could.

However, I saw that the poor fellow was most terribly scared. I comforted him as well as I could, and told him I was in as much danger as he, and that they would eat me as well as him.

"But," said I, "Friday, we must resolve to fight them. Can you fight, Friday?"

"Me shoot," said he, "but there come many great number."

"No matter for that," said I. "Our guns will frighten those that we do not kill." I asked him whether, if I resolved to defend him, he would defend me, and stand by me, and do just as I bade him.

He said, "Me die when you bid die, master."

I made him take the two fowling pieces, and load them with swan shot, as big as small pistol bullets. Then I took four muskets and loaded them with two slugs and five small bullets each, and my two pistols I loaded with a brace of bullets each. I hung my great sword, as usual, naked by my side, and gave Friday his hatchet.

When I had thus prepared myself I took my perspective glass and went up to the side of the hill to see what I could discover. I found quickly by my glass that there were twenty-one savages, three prisoners, and three canoes. Their whole business seemed to be a triumphant banquet upon these three human bodies.

They were landed, not where they had been when

Friday made his escape, but nearer to my creek, where
the shore was low, and where a thick wood came
close almost down to the sea. This, with the abhorrence of the inhuman errand these wretches came
about, so filled me with indignation, that I came down
to Friday, and told him I was resolved to go down
to them and kill them all, and asked him if he would
stand by me. He had now gotten over his fright,
and was very cheerful. He told me as before, "Me
die when you bid die."

I entered the wood with all possible wariness and
silence (Friday following close at my heels) and
marched till I came to the skirt of the wood, on the
side which was next to them, but one corner of the
wood lay between me and them. Here I called softly
to Friday, and showing him a great tree which was
just at the corner of the wood, I bade him go to the
tree, and bring me word if he could see there plainly
what they were doing. He did so, and came immediately back to me, and told me that they might be
plainly viewed there. They were all about the fire,
eating the flesh of one of their prisoners, and another
lay bound upon the sand, a little from them, whom,
he said, they would kill next. That fired the very
soul within me. He told me that it was not one of
their own nation, but one of the bearded men whom
he had told me of, that came to their country in the
boat. I was filled with horror at the very naming of
the white, bearded man, and, going to the tree, I saw
plainly by my glass a white man, who lay upon the

beach with his hands and feet tied. He was a European, and had clothes on.

There was another tree, and a little thicket beyond it, about fifty yards nearer to them than the place where I was, which I saw I might reach undiscovered. Then I should be within half a shot of them. So I withheld my passion, and, going back about twenty paces, I got behind some bushes, which held all the way till I came to the other tree, and then I came to a little rising ground, which gave me a full view of them, at the distance of about eighty yards.

I had now not a moment to lose, for nineteen of the dreadful wretches sat upon the ground, all close huddled together, and had just sent the other two to butcher the poor Christian, and bring him, perhaps limb by limb, to their fire. Already they had stooped down to untie the bands at his feet.

I turned to Friday. "Now, Friday," said I, "do as I bid you."

Friday said he would.

"Then, Friday," said I, "do exactly as you see me do; fail in nothing."

So I set down one of the muskets and the fowling piece upon the ground, and Friday did the same with his. With the other musket I took my aim at the savages, bidding him to do the same. I asked him if he was ready, and he said, "Yes."

"Then fire at them," said I, and at the same moment I fired also.

Friday took his aim so much better than I, that on

the side he shot he killed two of them and wounded three more; on my side, I killed one and wounded two. They were in a dreadful consternation. All of them who were not hurt jumped to their feet immediately, but they did not know which way to run or which way to look, for they knew not from whence their destruction came. Friday kept his eyes close upon me, so that, as I bade him, he might observe what I did. As soon as the first shot was made, I threw down the piece and took up the fowling piece, and Friday did the same. He saw me cock and take aim and he did the same again.

"Are you ready, Friday?" said I.

"Yes," said he.

"Let fly, then," said I, and with that I fired again among the amazed wretches, and so did Friday. As our pieces were now loaded with what I call swan shot, or small pistol bullets, we found only two drop, but so many were wounded that they ran about yelling and screaming like mad creatures, all bloody and wounded most of them. Three more fell quickly after, but they were not quite dead.

"Now, Friday," said I, laying down the discharged pieces and taking up the musket, which was yet loaded, "follow me." Upon this I rushed out of the wood and showed myself, and Friday followed close at my heels. As soon as I perceived that they saw me, I shouted as loud as I could, and bade Friday do so, too. Running as fast as I could, which, by the way, was not very fast, I made directly toward the poor

victim, who was, as I said, lying upon the beach, between the place where they sat and the sea. The two
butchers, who were just going to work with him, had
left him at the surprise of our first fire and fled, in a
terrible fright, to the seaside, and had jumped into a
canoe. Three more of the rest did the same. I turned
to Friday, and bade him step forward and fire at them.
He understood me immediately, and, running about
forty yards to be nearer them, he shot at them, and
I thought he had killed them all, for I saw them all
fall in a heap in the boat, though I saw two of them
up again quickly. However, he killed two of them,
and wounded the third, so that he lay in the bottom
of the boat as if he had been dead.

While Friday fired at them, I pulled out my knife
and cut the flags that bound the poor victim. Loosing
his hands and feet, I lifted him up, and asked him, in
the Portuguese tongue, what he was. He answered
in Latin, "Christianus," but he was so weak and faint,
that he could scarcely stand or speak. I took my
bottle out of my pocket and gave it to him, making
signs that he should drink, which he did, and I gave
him a piece of bread, which he ate. Then I asked
him what countryman he was, and he said, "Espagni-
ole." Being a little recovered, he let me know, by all
the signs he could possibly make, how much he was
in my debt for his deliverance. I said, in as good
Spanish as I could, "We will talk afterward, but we
must fight now; if you have any strength left, take the
pistol and sword and lay about you." He took them

very thankfully, and no sooner had he the arms in
his hands, but, as if they had put new vigor into him,
he flew upon his murderers like a fury, and had cut
two of them in pieces in an instant, for they were so
surprised and frightened that they could make no re-
sistance, nor attempt to escape.

I kept my piece in my hand still, without firing,
being willing to keep my charge ready, because I had
given the Spaniard my pistol and sword. I called to
Friday, and bade him run up to the tree from which

we had first fired, and bring the arms which lay there, that had been discharged, which he quickly did. Then giving him my musket, I sat down to load all the rest again, and bade them come to me when they wanted. While I was loading these pieces, there happened a fierce engagement between the Spaniard and one of the savages, who made at him with one of their great wooden swords, the same weapon that was to have killed him before, if I had not prevented it. The Spaniard, who was very bold, though weak, had fought this Indian a good while, and had cut him two great wounds on his head, but the savage, being a stout, lusty fellow, closing in with him, had thrown him down, and was wringing my sword out of his hand, when the Spaniard, though undermost, wisely quitted the sword, drew the pistol from his girdle, and shot him dead.

Friday, accompanied by the Spaniard, now pursued the fleeing savages with such deadly purpose that only three of them were able to reach their canoe. These were so badly wounded that I doubted if they would be able to row long enough to reach their home. Even so, I decided to follow them, but when I was in the other canoe I was surprised to find a poor savage lying there alive, bound hand and foot, as the Spaniard had been, for the slaughter. He was almost dead with fear, not knowing what the matter was, for he had not been able to look up over the side of the boat; he was tied so hard, neck and heels, and had been tied so long, that he had little life in him.

I immediately cut the twisted flags, or rushes, that bound him, and would have helped him up, but he could not stand or speak, but groaned, most piteously, believing, it seems, still, that he was only unbound in order to be killed. When Friday came, I bade him speak to him, and tell him of his deliverance, and pulling out my bottle, made him give the poor wretch a dram, which, with the news of his being delivered, revived him, and he sat up in the boat. But when Friday came to hear him speak, and looked in his face, it would have moved anyone to tears to have seen how Friday kissed him, embraced him, hugged him, cried, laughed, hallooed, jumped about, danced, sang, than cried again, wrung his hands, beat his own face and head, and then sang and jumped about again, like a distracted creature. It was a good while before I could make him speak to me, or tell me what was the matter, but when he came a little to himself he said that it was his father.

It is not easy for me to express how it moved me, to see what ecstasy and filial affection had worked in this poor savage at the sight of his father, and at the thought of his being delivered from death. Nor indeed can I describe half the extravagance of his affection after this, for he went into the boat and out of the boat a great many times. When he went in to him, he would sit down by him, open his breast, and hold his father's head close to his bosom half an hour together, to nourish it. Then he would take his arms and ankles, which were numbed and stiff with the binding, and chafe and rub them with his hands.

Friday was so busy about his father that I could not find it in my heart to take him off for some time, but after I thought he could leave him a little, I called him to me, and he came jumping and laughing, and pleased to the highest extreme. Then I asked him if he had given his father any bread. He shook his head, and said, "None: ugly dog eat all up self." So I gave him a cake of bread, out of a little pouch I carried on purpose. I also gave him a dram for himself, but he would not taste it, but carried it to his father. I had in my pocket also two or three bunches of my raisins, so I gave him a handful of them for his father. He had no sooner given his father these raisins than I saw him come out of the boat, and run away as if he had been bewitched. He ran at such a rate (for he was the swiftest-footed fellow that ever I saw) that he was out of sight, as it were, in an instant, and though I called and hallooed after him, it was all one. Away he went, and in a quarter of an hour I saw him come back again, though not so fast as he went. As he came near I found that his pace was slacker because he had something in his hand.

When he came to me, I found that he had been quite home for an earthen jug, or pot, to bring his father some fresh water and that he had brought two more cakes or loaves of bread. The bread he gave me, but the water he carried to his father. It revived his father more than all the rum or spirits I had given him, for he was just fainting with thirst.

When his father had drunk, I called Friday to know if there was any water left. He said, "Yes," and I bade him to give it to the poor Spaniard, who was as much in want of it as his father, and I sent one of the cakes that Friday had brought to the Spaniard, too, who was indeed very weak. He was reposing himself upon a green place, under the shade of a tree, and his limbs were also very stiff, and very much swelled with the rude bandage he had been tied with. When I saw that, upon Friday's coming up to him with the water, he sat up and drank, and took the bread and began to eat, I went up to him and gave him a handful of raisins. He looked up in my face with all the tokens of gratitude and thankfulness that could appear in any countenance. He was so weak, notwithstanding the way that he had exerted himself in the fight, that he could not stand upon his feet. He tried to do it two or three times, but was really not able, his ankles were so swelled and so painful to him. I bade him sit still, and caused Friday to rub his ankles, and bathe them with rum, as he had done his father's.

I observed that the poor, affectionate creature, every two minutes, or perhaps less, all the while that he was here, turned his head to look for his father. At last he missed him. At once he started up, and without speaking a word, flew with such swiftness to him, that one could scarcely perceive his feet touching the ground as he went, but when he reached him he found that he had only laid himself down to ease his limbs. So Friday came back to me presently, and I then told

him to help the Spaniard to the boat. He took him
upon his back, and carried him beside his father in the
boat, and stepped out again, launched the boat off,
and paddled it along the shore faster than I could walk,
though the wind blew pretty hard, too. He brought
them safely into our creek, and leaving them in the
boat, ran away to get the other canoe. As he passed
me, I spoke to him, and asked him whither he went.
He told me, "Go fetch more boat." So away he
went, like the wind, for surely never man or horse
ran like him. He had the other canoe in the creek
almost as soon as I got to it by land. He took me
over, and then went to help our new guests out of
the boat, which he did, but they were neither of them
able to walk, so that poor Friday knew not what to do.

At last, we made a kind of handbarrow to lay them
on, and Friday and I carried them up both together
upon it between us. But when we got them to the
outside of our wall, or fortification, we were at a worse
loss than before, for it was impossible to get them
over, and I was resolved not to break it down. So
we set to work again, and in about two hours' time
Friday and I had made a very handsome tent, covered
with old sails and boughs of trees. It was in the space
outside our outer fence, and between that and the
grove of young wood which I had planted. Here we
made them two beds of such things as I had, good rice
straw, with blankets laid upon it to lie on, and another
to cover them on each bed.

My island was now peopled, and I thought myself very rich in subjects. It was a merry reflection which I frequently made, how like a king I looked. First of all, the whole country was my own mere property, so that I had an undoubted right of dominion. Secondly, my people were perfectly subjected. I was the absolute lord and lawgiver; they all owed their lives to me, and were ready to lay down their lives, if there had been occasion of it, for me. It was remarkable, too, that I had but three subjects, and they were of three different religions. My man Friday was a Protestant; his father was a pagan and a cannibal; the Spaniard was a papist. However, I allowed liberty of conscience to all my subjects.

As soon as I had made my two weak, rescued prisoners secure, and given them shelter, and a place to rest upon, I began to think of making some provision for them. The first thing I did was to order Friday to take a yearling goat, out of my particular flock, to be killed. Then I cut off the hinder quarter, and chopping it into small pieces, I set Friday to work boiling and stewing. Thus we made them a very good dish of flesh and broth, and we all enjoyed it and ate heartily.

After we had dined, or rather supped, I ordered Friday to take one of the canoes and go and get our muskets and other firearms from the place of battle. The next day I ordered him to go and bury the dead bodies of the savages, which lay open to the sun, and would presently be offensive. I also ordered him to bury the horrid remains of their barbarous feast. All these things he punctually performed.

I then began to enter into a little conversation with my two new subjects. First I set Friday to inquire of his father what he thought of the escape of the savages in that canoe, and whether we might expect a return of them with a power too great for us to resist. His first opinion was that the savages in the boat never could live out the storm which blew that night they went off, but must be drowned, or driven south to those other shores, where they were sure to be devoured. As to what they would do, if they came on shore, he said that he knew not, but it was his opinion that they were so dreadfully frightened with the manner of their being attacked, the noise and the fire, that he believed that they would tell their people that they were all killed by thunder and lightning, and not by the hand of man, and that the two which appeared (namely, Friday and I) were two heavenly spirits and furies come down to destroy them, and not with weapons. And this old savage was right, for though they escaped the sea, they gave such dreadful accounts in their own country (as I heard afterward), that they never ventured to my island again.

But I was under continual apprehensions for some time, and kept upon my guard, I and all my army, for, as there were now four of us, I would have ventured upon a hundred of them in the open field.

In a little time, however, no more canoes appearing,

the fear of their coming wore off, and I began to take into consideration my former thoughts of a voyage to the mainland. I was likewise assured by Friday's father that I might depend upon good usage from their nation, on his account, if I would go.

One day I had a serious discourse with the Spaniard, and learned that there were sixteen more of his countrymen and Portuguese who had been cast away and had made their escape to that side. The Spaniard told me that they lived there at peace indeed with the savages, but were very sore put to it for necessaries, and indeed for life. I asked him all the particulars of their voyage, and found that they were a Spanish ship, bound from the Rio de la Plata to Havana. They had been directed to leave their loading there, which was chiefly hides and silver, and to bring back what European goods they could meet with there. They had had five Portuguese seamen on board, whom they took out of another wreck. Five of their own men were drowned when first their ship was lost and those that escaped passed through infinite dangers and hazards, and arrived, almost starved, on the cannibal coast, where they expected to be devoured every moment.

He told me that they had some arms with them, but they were perfectly useless, for they had neither powder nor ball. The washing of the sea had spoiled all their powder but a little, which they had used when they first landed to provide themselves some food.

I asked him if they had formed no design of making an escape. He said that they had had many consultations about it, but having neither vessel, nor tools to build one, nor provisions of any kind, their counsels always ended in tears and despair. I asked him how he thought they would receive a proposal from me, which might tend toward an escape, and, whether, if they were all here, it might not be done.

He told me that they were all under the greatest distress imaginable, and if I would undertake their relief, they would live and die by me.

Upon these assurances, I resolved to venture to relieve them, if possible, and to send the old savage and the Spaniard over to them to treat. But when he had gotten all things in readiness to go, the Spaniard himself started an objection, which had so much prudence in it on the one hand, and so much sincerity on the other, that I could not but be well satisfied in it. By his advice I put off the deliverance of his comrades for at least half a year. He had been with us now about a month, during which time I had let him see in what manner I had provided, with the assistance of Providence, for my support. He saw what stock of corn and rice I had laid up, which, while it was more than sufficient for myself, was not sufficient, at least without good husbandry, for my family, now that it was increased to the number of four. Much less would it be sufficient if his countrymen, who were, as he said, fourteen, should come over. Least of all, would it be sufficient to victual our vessel, if we should build one, for a voyage to any of the Christian colonies of America. So he told me that he thought it would be more advisable to let him and the two others dig and cultivate more land, as much as I could spare seed to sow. Then, if we should wait another harvest, we might have a supply of grain for his countrymen, when they should come. Want might be a temptation to them to disagree, or not think themselves delivered, otherwise than out of one difficulty into another.

The Spaniard's caution was so seasonable, and his advice so good, that I could not but be very well pleased with his proposal, as well as satisfied with his fidelity. So we fell to digging, all four of us, as well as the wooden tools we were furnished with permitted. In about a month's time, by the end of which it was seed time, we had gotten enough land cured, and trimmed up to sow twenty-two bushels of barley on, and sixteen jars of rice, which was, in short, all the seed we had to spare.

At the same time, I contrived to increase my little flock of tame goats as much as I could, and to this purpose I made Friday and the Spaniard go out one day, and myself with Friday the next day, for we took our turns. By this means, we got about twenty young kids to breed up with the rest, for, whenever we shot the dam we saved the kids, and added them to our flock. But, above all, the season for curing the grapes coming on, I caused such a prodigious quantity to be hung up in the sun, that I believe, had we been at Alicant, where raisins are cured, we should have filled sixty or eighty barrels. These with our bread formed a great part of our food.

It was now harvest, and our crop was in good order. It was not the most plentiful increase I had seen in the island, but it was enough to answer our end. From our twenty-two bushels of barley, we brought in and threshed out more than two hundred and twenty bushels, and an equal proportion of the rice, which was store enough for our food until the next harvest, though all the fourteen Spaniards had been on shore with me. If we had been ready for a voyage, it would very plentifully have victualed our ship to have carried us to any part of America. When we had thus stored our grain, we fell to work to make great wicker baskets in which we kept it. The Spaniard was very handy and dexterous at this part.

And now, having a full supply of food for all the guests I expected, I gave the Spaniard leave to go over to the mainland, to see what he could do with those whom he had left behind him there. I gave him strict charge not to bring any man with him who would not first swear, in the presence of himself and the old savage, that he would in no way injure, fight with, or attack the person he should find in the island, who was so kind as to send for him to deliver him. Each man was to swear that he would stand by and defend that person against all such attempts, and wherever he went, he would be entirely under and subjected to his command. This should be put in writing, and signed by all the men.

Under these instructions, the Spaniard and the old savage went away in one of the canoes which they came in, when they were brought as prisoners to be devoured by the savages. I gave each of them a musket and about eight charges of powder and ball, charging them to be very careful of both, and not to use either of them but upon very urgent occasions.

This was a cheerful work, being the first measures used by me, in view of my deliverance, for now twenty-seven years and some days. I gave them provisions of bread and dried grapes, sufficient for themselves for many days, and sufficient for all the countrymen for about eight days. Wishing them a good voyage, I let them go, after I had agreed with them about a signal they should hang out at their return, by which I should know them at a distance before they came on shore.

They went away, with a fair gale, on the day that the moon was at the full, by my account, in the month of October.

I had waited for them no less than eight days, when a strange and unforeseen occurrence intervened, of which the like has not, perhaps, been heard in history.

Deliverance ~

I was fast asleep in my hut one morning, when my man Friday came running in to me, and called aloud, "Master, master, they are come, they are come!" I jumped up, and, regardless of danger, went out, as soon as I could get my clothes on, through my little grove. I went without my arms, which it was not my custom to do. I was surprised, when, turning my eyes to the sea, I presently saw a boat, at about a league and a half distance, standing in for the shore, with a shoulder-of-mutton sail, as they call it. The wind was blowing pretty fair to bring them in. Also, I observed that they did not come from that side which the shore lay on, but from the southernmost end of the island. Upon this I called Friday in and bade him lie close, for these were not the people we looked for, and we did not know yet whether they were friends or enemies. In the next place, I went in to get my perspective glass, to see what I could make of them. When I had taken the ladder out, I climbed up to the top of the hill, as I used to do when I was apprehensive of anything, to take my view plainer, without being discovered. I had scarcely set my foot on the hill, when my eye plainly discovered a ship lying at anchor, at about two leagues and a half distance from me, SSE., but not more than a league and a half from the shore. It appeared plainly to be an English ship, and the boat an English longboat.

I had not been long in this position, when I saw the boat draw near the shore, as if they looked for a creek to thrust in at, for the convenience of landing. However, as they did not come quite far enough, they did not see the little inlet where I formerly landed my rafts, but ran their boat on shore upon the beach, at about half a mile from me, which was very fortunate for me. Otherwise they would have landed just, as I may say, at my door, and would soon have beaten me out of my castle, and, perhaps, have plundered me of all I had.

When they were on shore, I was fully satisfied they were Englishmen, at least most of them; one or two I thought were Dutch, but they did not prove so. There were, in all, eleven men. Three I found were unarmed, and (as I thought) bound. When the first four or five of them had jumped on shore, they took these three out of the boat as prisoners. One I could perceive was using the most passionate gestures of en- treaty, affliction, and despair. The other two lifted up their hands sometimes, and appeared concerned indeed, but not so much as the first.

I was perfectly confounded at the sight, and knew not what the meaning of it could be.

Friday called out to me, in English, as well as he could, "O master, you see English mans eat prisoners as well as savage mans."

"Why," said I, "do you think they are going to eat them, then?"

"Yes," says Friday, "they will eat them."

"No, no," said I, "Friday, I am afraid they will murder them, indeed, but you may be sure that they will not eat them."

All this while I had no thought of what the matter really was, but expected every moment that the three prisoners would be killed. Once I saw one of the villains lift a great cutlass or sword to strike one of the poor men, and I expected every moment to see him fall. I wished heartily now for my Spaniard and the savage that had gone with him. I wished, too, that I had a way to come undiscovered within shot of the newcomers, that I might rescue the three men, for the sailors had no firearms that I saw.

After the three men had been outrageously used by the insolent seamen, I saw that the fellows ran scattering about the land, as if they wanted to see the country. I observed, also, that the three other men had liberty to go where they pleased, but that they sat down all three upon the ground, very pensive, and looked like men in despair.

It was just at the top of high water when these people came on shore, and they stood parleying with the prisoners they brought, and they rambled about to see what kind of place they were in so long that they carelessly stayed till the tide was spent, and the water had ebbed considerably away, leaving the boat aground. They had left two men in the boat, who, as I found afterward, had drunk a little too much brandy and had fallen asleep. However, one of them wakening sooner than the other, and finding the boat too fast aground for him to stir her, hallooed for the rest, who were straggling about. Upon this they all soon came to the boat, but it was past all their strength to launch her, for the boat was very heavy, and the shore on that side was a soft, oozy sand, almost like a quicksand. Under these circumstances, like true seamen, who are, perhaps, the least of all mankind given to forethought, they gave it up, and away they strolled about the country again. I heard one of them say aloud to another (calling them off from the boat), "Why, let her alone, Jack, can't ye! She'll float next tide." By this I was fully confirmed what country-men they were.

In the meantime, I fitted myself up for a battle, as before, though with more caution, knowing that I had to do with another kind of enemy than I had at first. I ordered Friday also to load himself with arms. I took myself two fowling pieces, and I gave him three muskets. My figure indeed was very fierce; I had my goat's-skin coat on, with the great cap I have mentioned, a naked sword by my side, two pistols in my belt, and a gun upon each shoulder.

It was my design not to have made any attempt until it was dark, but about two o'clock, in the heat of the day, I found that they had all gone straggling into the woods, and, as I thought, had all lain down to sleep. The three, poor, distressed men, too anxious for their condition to get any sleep, had, however, sat down under the shelter of a great tree, at about a quarter of a mile from me, and, as I thought, out of sight of any of the rest.

Upon this I resolved to discover myself to them, and learn something of their condition. Immediately I marched toward them, with my man Friday at a good distance behind me. He was as formidably armed as I, but he did not make quite so staring a specter-like figure as I did. I came as near them undiscovered as I could, and then, before any of them saw me, I called aloud to them, in Spanish, "What are ye, gentlemen?"

They started up at the noise, but were ten times more confounded when they saw me, and the uncouth figure I made. They made no answer at all, but I thought I perceived them just going to fly from me, so I spoke to them in English.

"Gentlemen," said I, "do not be surprised at me; perhaps you may have a friend near you when you do not expect it."

"He must be sent directly from heaven, then," said one of them very gravely to me, and pulling off his hat at the same time, "for our condition is past the help of man."

"All help is from heaven, sir," said I, "but can you

put a stranger in the way how to help you? You seem to be in some great distress. I saw you when you landed, and when you seemed to make application to the brutes that came with you, I saw one lift his sword to kill you."

The poor man, with tears running down his face, and trembling, looking like one astonished, returned, "Am I talking to God or man? Is it a real man or an angel?"

"Be in no fear about that, sir," said I. "If God had sent an angel to relieve you, he would have come better clothed, and armed after another manner, than you see me. Pray lay aside your fears. I am a man, an Englishman, and disposed to assist you, you see. I have one servant only, but we have arms and ammunition. Tell us freely, can we serve you? What is your case?"

"Our case, sir," said he, "is too long to tell you, while our murderers are so near, but, in short, sir, I was commander of that ship. My men have mutinied against me. They have been with difficulty prevailed upon not to murder me, and, at last, have set me on shore in this desolate place, with these two men with me, one my mate, the other a passenger. We expected to perish here, believing the place to be uninhabited. Indeed, we know not yet what to think of it."

"Where are those brutes, your enemies?" said I. "Do you know where they are gone?"

"There they are, sir," said he, pointing to a thicket

of trees. "My heart trembles for fear they have seen us, and heard you speak. If they have, they will murder us all."

"Have they any firearms?" I asked.

He answered, "They had only two pieces, and one which they left in the boat."

"Well, then," said I, "leave the rest to me. I see they are asleep. It is an easy thing to kill them all, but shall we rather take them prisoners?"

He told me that there were two desperate villains among them that it was scarcely safe to show any mercy to, but if they were secured, he believed all the rest would return to their duty. I asked him which they were. He told me that he could not, at that distance, describe them, but he would obey my orders in anything I would direct.

"Well," said I, "let us retreat out of their view or hearing, lest they awake, and we will resolve farther." So they willingly went back with me, till the woods covered us from them.

"Look you, sir," said I, "if I venture upon your deliverance, are you willing to make two conditions with me?"

He anticipated my proposals, by telling me that both he and the ship, if recovered, should be wholly directed and commanded by me in everything. If the ship was not recovered, he would live and die with me, in whatsoever part of the world I would send him. The two others said the same.

"Well," said I, "my conditions are but two. In

the first place, while you stay on this island with me, you will not pretend to any authority here. If I put arms in your hands, you will, upon all occasions, give them up to me. You will do no harm to me or mine, upon this island, and, in the meantime, you will be governed by my orders. In the second place, if the ship is, or may be, recovered, you will carry me and my man to England passage free."

He gave me all the assurances that the invention and faith of man could devise, that he would comply with these most reasonable demands, and, besides, would owe his life to me, and acknowledge it, upon all occasions, as long as he lived.

"Well, then," said I, "here are three muskets for you, with powder and ball. Tell me next what you think is proper to be done."

He showed all the testimony of his gratitude that he was able, but offered to be wholly guided by me. I told him that I thought it was hard venturing anything, but the best method I could think of was to fire upon them at once, as they lay. If any were not killed at the first volley, and offered to submit, we might save them, and so put it wholly upon God's providence to direct the shot.

He said, very modestly, that he was loath to kill them, if he could help it, but that those two were incorrigible villains, and had been the authors of all the mutiny in the ship, and if they escaped we should be undone still, for they would go on board and bring the whole ship's company, and destroy us all.

"Well, then," said I, "necessity legitimates my advice; for it is the only way to save our lives."

However, seeing him still cautious of shedding blood, I told him they should go themselves, and manage as they found convenient.

In the middle of this discourse we heard some of them awake, and soon after we saw two of them on their feet. I asked him if they were the men who, he had said, were the heads of the mutiny.

He said, "No."

"Well, then," said I, "you may let them escape. Providence seems to have awakened them on purpose to save themselves. Now," said I, "if the rest escape you, it is your fault."

Animated with this, he took the musket I had given him in his hand, and a pistol in his belt, and his two comrades with him, each man a piece in his hand. The two men who were with him, going first, made some noise, at which one of the seamen, who was awake, turned about, and seeing them coming, cried out to the rest. It was too late then, for the moment he cried out, the two men fired, the captain wisely reserving his own piece. They had so well aimed their shot at the men they knew that one of them was killed on the spot, and the other very much wounded, but, not being dead, he started up upon his feet, and called eagerly for help to the other. The captain, stepping to him, told him that it was too late to cry for help, he should call upon God to forgive his villainy, and, with that

word, knocked him down with the stock of his musket, so that he never spoke more.

There were three more in the company, and one
of them was also slightly wounded. By this time I
was come, and when they saw their danger, and that it
was in vain to resist, they begged for mercy. The
captain told them he would spare their lives if they
would give him any assurance of their abhorrence of
the treachery they had been guilty of, and would
swear to be faithful to him in recovering the ship, and
afterward in carrying her back to Jamaica, from
whence they came. They gave him all the protesta-
tions of their sincerity that could be desired, and he
was willing to believe them, and spare their lives,
which I was not against. However, I obliged him to
keep them bound, hand and foot, while they were
upon the island.

While this was doing I sent Friday, with the captain's mate, to the boat, with orders to secure her, and
bring away the oars and sail, which they did. By and
by, three straggling men, that were parted from the
rest, came back again upon hearing the guns fired,
and seeing their captain, who was before their prisoner, now their conqueror, they submitted to being
bound also.

It now remained that the captain and I should inquire into one another's circumstances. I began first,
and told him my whole history, which he heard with
amazed attention. He was particularly astounded at

the wonderful manner of my being furnished with
provisions and ammunition, and, indeed, as my story
is a whole collection of wonders, it affected him
deeply. When he reflected from thence upon himself, and how I seemed to have been preserved there
on purpose to save his life, the tears ran down his face,
and he could not speak a word more.

After this communication was at an end, I carried
him and his two men into my apartment, leading them
in just where I came out, at the top of the house. I
refreshed them with such provisions as I had, and
showed them all the contrivances I had made during
my long stay in this place.

All I showed them, all I said to them, was perfectly
amazing, but, above all, the captain admired my fortification, and how perfectly I had concealed my retreat
with a grove of trees. They had been planted now
nearly twenty years. The trees grew much faster
than in England, so that it had become a little wood,
and so thick that it was impassable except at that one
side where I had reserved my little winding passage
into it. This I told him was my castle and my residence, but that I had a seat in the country, as most
princes have, whither I could retreat upon occasion,
and I would show him that too another time. At
present, however, our business was to consider how to
recover the ship. He agreed with me as to that, but
he told me that he was perfectly at a loss what measures to take, because there were still six-and-twenty

hands on board. They had entered into a cursed conspiracy, by which they had all forfeited their lives to the law, and they would be hardened in it now by desperation, and would carry it on, knowing that if they were captured they should be brought to the gallows as soon as they came to England, or to any of the English colonies. Therefore there would be no use attacking them with so small a number as we were.

I mused for some time upon what he had said, and found that it was a very rational conclusion. It occurred to me, too, that, in a little while, the ship's crew, wondering what had become of their comrades, and of the boat, would certainly come on shore, in their other boat, to look for them. Then perhaps, they might come armed, and be too strong for us. This, the captain agreed, was likely.

Upon this, I told him that the first thing we had to do was to stave the boat, which lay upon the beach, so that they might not carry her off, and, taking everything out of her, leave her so useless as not to be fit to float. Accordingly, we went on board, took the arms which were left on board out of her, and whatever else we found there, which was a bottle of brandy, and another of rum, a few biscuit cakes, a horn of powder, and a great lump of sugar, in a piece of canvas. The sugar was five or six pounds. All this was very welcome to me, especially the sugar, which I had been without many years.

When we had carried all these things on shore, we

knocked a great hole in her bottom, so that if they came strong enough to master us, yet they could not carry off the boat.

Indeed, it was not much in my thoughts that we could recover the ship, but my view was, that if they went away without the boat, I did not much question to make her fit again to carry us away to the Leeward Islands, and call upon our friends the Spaniards on my way.

While we were thus preparing our plans, we first, by main strength, heaved the boat up on the beach, so high that the tide would not float her off at high-water mark. Besides, we broke a hole in her bottom too big to be quickly stopped. While we sat musing what we should do, we heard the ship fire a gun, and saw her make a waft* with her ancient,† as a signal for the boat, to come on board. When no boat stirred, they fired several times, making other signals.

At last, when all their signals and firings proved fruitless, and they found that the boat did not stir, we saw them (by the help of my glasses) hoist another boat off, and row toward the shore. We found, as they approached, that there were no less than ten men in her, and that they had firearms with them.

As the ship lay almost two leagues from the shore, we had a full view of them as they came. The captain knew the persons and characters of all the men in the boat, of whom he said there were three very honest

---

* Waft is a nautical term, meaning a signal made with a flag or a pennant.

† Ancient is an archaic word, meaning a flag flown on a ship.

fellows, who, he was sure, were led into this conspiracy by the rest, being overpowered and frightened.
As for the boatswain, who, it seems, was the chief
officer among them, and all the rest, they were as out-
rageous as any of the ship's crew, and were, no doubt,
made desperate in their new enterprise.

We had, upon the first sign of the boat's coming
from the ship, separated our prisoners and secured
them effectually. Two of them, of whom the captain was less assured than ordinary, I sent with Friday,
and one of the three delivered men, to my cave, where
they were remote enough, and out of danger of being
heard or discovered, or of finding their way out of the
woods. They left them bound, but gave them provisions, and promised them, if they continued there
quietly, to give them their liberty in a day or two, but
they assured them that if they attempted their escape,
they should be put to death without mercy. The
prisoners promised faithfully to bear their confinement
with patience.

The other prisoners had better usage. Two of them
were kept bound indeed, because the captain did not
like to trust them, but the other two were taken into
my service, upon their captain's recommendation, and
upon their solemnly engaging to live and die with us.

As soon as the newcomers got to the place where
their other boat lay, they ran their boat into the beach,
and came all on shore, hauling the boat up after them,
which I was glad to see. I had been afraid that they
would leave the boat, and anchor some distance from

the shore, with some hands in her to guard her, so that we should not be able to seize the boat.

When they were on shore they all ran to the other boat, and it was easy to see that they were greatly surprised to find her stripped, and a great hole in the bottom. After this, they set up a great shout, but it was all to no purpose. Then they came all close in a ring, and fired a volley of their small arms, which indeed we heard, and the echoes made the woods ring, but it was all one. Those in the cave we were sure could not hear, and those in our keeping, though they heard it well enough, yet dared give no answer to them.

They were so surprised at this, as they told us afterward, that they resolved to go on board their ship again, and let their friends there know that the men were all murdered, and the longboat staved. Accordingly, they immediately launched their boat again, and got all of them on board.

The captain was terribly amazed, and even confounded at this, believing they would go on board the ship again, and set sail, giving their comrades up for lost. In that case, he would still lose the ship, which he was in hopes we should have recovered. Before long, however, he was as much frightened the other way.

They had not put off far with the boat, when we perceived them all coming on shore again. They left three men in the boat, and the rest went up into the country to look for their fellows. This was a great

disappointment to us, for now we were at a loss what
to do. Our seizing those seven men on shore would
be no advantage to us if we let the boat escape, because the others would then row away to the ship,
and the rest of them would be sure to weigh and set
sail, and so our hope of recovering the ship would be
lost. However, we had no remedy but to wait and
see what the issue of things might present. The seven
men came on shore, and the three who remained in
the boat put her off to a good distance from the shore,
and came to an anchor, to wait for them, so that it
was impossible for us to come at them in the boat.

Those that came on shore kept close together,
marching toward the top of the little hill, under which
my dwelling lay, and we could see them plainly,
though they could not perceive us. When they came
to the brow of the hill, where they could see a great
way into the valleys and woods which lay toward the
northeast part, and where the island lay lowest, they
shouted till they were weary, and then they sat down
to consider the situation. Had they gone to sleep
there, as the other party did, they would have done
the job for us, but they were too full of apprehension
of danger to venture to go to sleep, though they could
not tell what the danger was.

The captain suggested that perhaps they would all
fire a volley again, to endeavor to make their fellows
hear, and then we could all sally upon them just at
the juncture when their pieces were all discharged,
and they would certainly yield, and we should have

them without bloodshed. I liked the proposal, provided it was done while we were near enough to come up to them before they could load their pieces again.

But this event did not happen, and we lay still a long time, very irresolute what course to take. At length I told him there was nothing to be done, in my opinion, till night. Then, if they did not return to the boat, perhaps we might use some stratagem to get those in the boat on shore.

We waited a great while very impatiently. When we finally saw them all start up, and march toward the sea we were uneasy. It seems that they had such dreadful apprehensions upon them of the danger of the place, that they resolved to go on board the ship again, give their companions up for lost, and so go on their intended voyage with the ship.

As soon as I perceived them going toward the shore, I imagined that they had given up their search, and were going back. The captain was ready to sink when I told him my thoughts, but I presently thought of a stratagem to bring them back again, which answered my end to a tittle.

I ordered Friday and the captain's mate to go over the little creek westward, toward the place where Friday was rescued, and at about half a mile distance, to halloo as loud as they could. As soon as they heard the seamen answer them, they were to return it, and then, keeping out of sight, take a round, and wheel about again to me by such ways as I directed.

The men were just going into the boat, when Friday and the mate hallooed, and they presently heard them, and answering, ran along the shore westward, toward the voice they heard.   They were stopped by the creek—the water being up, they could not get over—and called for the boat to come and set them over, as, indeed, I had expected.

When they had set themselves over, I observed that they took one of the three men out of her, and left only two there.   The boat they fastened to a stump of a little tree on the shore.

This was what I wished for.   Leaving Friday and the captain's mate to their business, I took the rest with me, and crossing the creek out of the sight of the men, we surprised them before they were aware. One of them was lying on the shore between sleeping and waking, and, as he was starting up, the captain, who was foremost, ran in upon him and knocked him down.   He then called to the man in the boat to yield or he was a dead man.

Very few arguments were needed to persuade a single man to yield, when he saw five men upon him, and his comrade knocked down.   Besides, this was, it seems, one of the three men who were not so hearty in the mutiny as the rest of the crew.   Therefore he was easily persuaded not only to yield, but afterward to join very sincerely with us.

In the meantime Friday and the captain's mate so well managed their business with the rest, that they drew them, by hallooing and answering, from one wood to another, till they not only heartily tired them, but left them where they were sure they could not get back before it was dark. Indeed Friday and the mate were heartily tired themselves also by the time they came back to us.

It was several hours after Friday came back to me before the men came back to their boat. We could hear the foremost of them long before they quite came up, calling to those behind to come along, and could hear them answer, and complain how lame and tired they were, which was very welcome news to us.

At length they came up to the boat, but it is impossible to express their confusion when they found the boat fast aground in the creek, and their two men gone. We could hear them telling one another that they had gotten into an enchanted island. They were sure that either there were inhabitants in it, and they should all be murdered, or else there were devils or spirits in it, and they should be carried away and devoured.

They hallooed again, and called their two comrades by their names, but got no answer. After some time, we could see by the little light there was that they were running about like men in despair. Sometimes they would go and sit down in the boat to rest themselves, then they would come on shore again, and walk about.

My men would have fallen upon them in the dark, but I was willing to spare them, and kill as few of them as I could. I was unwilling to risk the killing of any of our men, knowing that the others were well armed. I resolved to wait and make sure of them, and drew my ambuscade nearer. I ordered Friday and the captain to creep upon their hands and knees, and get as near them as they possibly could before they offered to fire.

They had not been long in that position when the boatswain, who was the principal ringleader, and had now shown himself the most dispirited of all the rest, walked toward them with two more of their crew. The captain was so eager at having the principal rogue so much in his power, that he could hardly have patience to let him come near enough to be sure of him, for he had only heard his voice before. When they came nearer, the captain and Friday, starting up on their feet, ley fly at them.

The boatswain was killed on the spot, the next was shot through the body, and fell just by him, though he did not die till an hour or two after, and the third ran for it.

At the noise of the fire, I immediately advanced with my whole army, which was now eight men: I, myself, generalissimo; Friday, my lieutenant general; the captain and his two men; the three prisoners of war, whom we had trusted with arms.

We came upon them indeed in the dark, so that they could not see our number. I made the man that they had left in the boat, who was now one of us, call them by name, to see if he could bring them to parley, which fell out just as we desired.

He called out as loud as he could to one of them. "Tom Smith! Tom Smith!"

Tom Smith answered immediately, "Is that Robinson?" for it seems that he knew his voice.

The other answered, "Ay, ay; for God's sake, Tom Smith, throw down your arms and yield, or you are all dead men this moment!"

"Whom must we yield to? Where are they?" says Tom Smith again.

"Here they are," says he. "Here is our captain, and fifty men with him, have been hunting you this two hours. The boatswain is killed, Will Frye is wounded, and I am a prisoner. If you do not yield, you are all lost."

"If they will give us quarter, then," says Tom Smith, "we will yield."

"I'll go and ask, if you promise to yield," says Robinson.

So he asked the captain, and the captain himself then called out, "You, Smith, you know my voice; if you lay down your arms immediately, and submit, you shall all have your lives, all but Will Atkins."

Upon this Will Atkins cried out, "For God's sake, captain, give me quarter! What have I done? They have all been as bad as I!" This was not true, for it seems that this Will Atkins was the first man that laid hold of the captain when they first mutinied. However, the captain told him that he must lay down his arms at discretion, and trust to the governor's mercy. By this he meant me, for they called me governor.

In a word, they all laid down their arms, and begged their lives. I sent the man that had parleyed with

them, and two more, who bound them all. Then my
great army of fifty men, which, with those three, were
in all but eight, came up and seized them all, and their
boat. I kept myself and one more out of sight, for
reasons of state.

Our next work was to repair the boat, and to think
of seizing the ship. The captain, now that he had
leisure to parley with them, expostulated with them
upon the villainy of their practices with him, and how
certainly it must bring them to misery and distress in
the end, and perhaps to the gallows.

They all appeared very penitent, and begged hard
for their lives. As for that, he told them that the governor was an Englishman, and that he might hang
them all there if he pleased. However, since he had
given them quarter, he supposed he would send them
to England, except Atkins, whom he was commanded
by the governor to advise to prepare for death, because he would be hanged in the morning. Though
this was all a fiction of his own, yet it had the desired
effect. Atkins fell upon his knees to beg the captain
to intercede with the governor for his life, and all the
rest begged of him, for God's sake, not to be sent to
England.

It now occurred to me that the time of our deliverance had come, and that it would be a most easy thing
to make these fellows help in getting possession of the
ship. So I retired in the dark from them, that they
might not see what kind of governor they had, and
called the captain to me. When I called, as at a good

distance, one of the men was ordered to speak again,
and to say to the captain, "Captain, the commander
calls for you," and presently the captain replied, "Tell
his excellency I am just coming." So they all believed
that the commander was just by with his fifty men.

Upon the captain's coming to me, I told him my
project for seizing the ship, which pleased him. We
resolved to put it in execution the next morning.

But in order to execute it with more art, and to be
sure of success, I told him that we must divide the
prisoners, and that he should go and take Atkins,
and two more of the worst of them, and send them
bound to the cave where the others lay. So Friday,
and the two men who came on shore with the captain,
conveyed them to the cave as to a prison. The others
I ordered to my bower, where they were bound, and
left secure enough.

To these, in the morning, I sent the captain, who
was to enter into a parley with them, to try them and
tell me whether he thought they might be trusted or
not, to go on board and surprise the ship. He talked
to them of the injury done him, and of the condition
they were brought to. He reminded them that though
the governor had given them quarter for their lives,
as to the present action, yet if they were sent to England, they would all be hanged in chains. He ended
by telling them that if they would join in so just an
attempt as to recover the ship, he would have the
governor's promise for their pardon.

Anyone may guess how readily such a proposal

would be accepted by men in their condition. They fell down on their knees to the captain, and promised, with solemn vows that they would be faithful to him to the last drop, and that they would owe their lives to him, and would go with him all over the world, and would own him for a father as long as they lived.

"Well," says the captain, "I must go and tell the governor what you say, and see what I can do to bring him to consent to it."

So he brought me an account of the temper he found them in, and that he verily believed they would be faithful. However, that we might be very secure, I told him he should go back again, and choose out five of them, and tell them that they should see he did not want men; but that he would take out those five to be his assistants, and that the governor would keep the other two, and the three that were sent prisoners to the castle (my cave), as hostages for the fidelity of those five. If they proved unfaithful in the execution, the five hostages should be hanged in chains alive upon the shore.

This looked severe, and convinced them that the governor was in earnest. However, they had no way left them but to accept it, and it was now the business of the prisoners, as much as of the captain, to persuade the other five to do their duty. Our strength was now thus ordered for the expedition: first, the captain, his mate, and the passenger; second, the two prisoners of the first gang, to whom, having their characters from the captain, I had given their liberty, and whom I had trusted with arms; third, the other two, whom I had kept bound in my bower, who were now released; fourth, these five, just released. There were twelve in all, besides the five whom we kept in the cave, as hostages for the fidelity of the others.

I asked the captain if he was willing to venture with those hands on board the ship. As for me and my man Friday, I did not think it proper for us to stir, having seven men left behind. It was employment enough for us to keep them apart, and supply them with victuals.

As to the five in the cave, I resolved to keep them fast, but Friday went twice a day to them, to supply them with necessaries. I made the other two carry provisions to a certain distance, where Friday was to take it.

When I showed myself to the two hostages, it was with the captain, who told them that I was the person whom the governor had ordered to look after them, and that it was the governor's pleasure they should not stir anywhere but by my direction. If they did, they should be brought to the castle and be laid in irons. In that way we never suffered them to see me as governor. I appeared as another person, and spoke of the governor, the garrison, the castle, and the like, upon all occasions.

The captain now had no difficulty before him but to furnish his two boats, stop the breach of one, and man them. He made his passenger captain of one, with four other men. He himself, with his mate and five more, went in the other. They contrived their business very well, for they came up to the ship about midnight. As soon as they came within call of the ship, he made Robinson hail them, and tell them that he had brought off the men and the boat, but that it was a long time before they had found them. He held them in chat till they came to the ship's side, when the captain and the mate, entering first with their arms, immediately knocked down the second mate and the carpenter with the butt end of their muskets, being very faithfully seconded by their men. They secured all the rest that were upon the main and quarter-decks, and began to fasten the hatches to keep them down who were below when the men from the other boat entering the forechains, secured the forecastle of the ship, and the scuttle which went down into the cookroom, making three men they found there prisoners. When this was done, and all safe upon the deck, the captain ordered the mate with three men to break into the roundhouse, where the new rebel captain lay. He, having taken alarm and gotten up, now stood with two men and a boy, having firearms in their hands. When the mate with a crowbar split open the door, the new captain and his men fired boldly among them, and wounded the mate with a musket ball, which broke his arm, and wounded two more of the men.

The mate calling for help, rushed, however, into the roundhouse, wounded as he was, and, with his pistol, shot the new captain through the head. The bullet entered at his mouth, and came out again behind one of his ears, so that he never spoke a word again. Upon this the rest yielded, and the ship was taken effectually, without any more lives lost. As soon as the ship was thus secured, the captain ordered seven guns to be fired, which was the signal agreed upon with me, to give me notice of his success, which, you may be sure, I was glad to hear. I had sat watching upon the shore for it till two o'clock in the morning.

Having heard the signal plainly, I laid me down, and being very much fatigued, I fell sound asleep. Shortly I was awakened by the noise of a gun, and, starting up, I heard a man call me by the name of "Governor," and presently I knew the captain's voice. I climbed up to the top of the hill, and there he stood. Pointing to the ship, he embraced me in his arms.

"My dear friend and deliverer," said he, "there's your ship, for she is all yours, and so are we, and all that belongs to her."

I cast my eyes to the ship, and there she rode, about half a mile off the shore, for they had weighed her anchor as soon as they were masters of her, and the weather being fair, had brought her to an anchor just against the mouth of a little creek. The tide being up, they had brought the pinnace in near the place where I had first landed my rafts, and so landed just at my door.

I was, at first, ready to sink down with surprise, for I saw my deliverance indeed visibly put into my hands, all things easy, and a large ship just ready to carry me away whither I pleased to go. He perceived my situation, and immediately pulled a bottle out of his pocket, and gave me a dram of cordial, which he had brought on purpose for me. After I drank it, I sat down upon the ground, and it was a good while before I could speak to him.

After some time I came to myself, and then I embraced him in my turn, as my deliverer, and we rejoiced together. I told him that I looked upon him as a man sent from heaven to deliver me, and that the whole transaction seemed to be a chain of wonders. Such things as these were the testimonies we had of a secret hand of Providence governing the world, and an evidence that the eyes of an infinite Power could search into the remotest corner of the world, and send help to the miserable whenever He pleased. I did not forget to return thanks to God for all His mercies.

When we had talked awhile, the captain told me that he had brought me some little refreshment, such as the ship afforded, and such as the wretches, who had been so long his masters, had not plundered him of. Upon this he called aloud to his men, and told them to bring the things ashore that were for the governor, and it was a splendid present. First, he had brought me a case of bottles full of cordial waters, six large bottles of Madeira wine, two pounds of excellent tobacco, twelve good pieces of the ship's beef, and six pieces of pork, with a bag of peas, and about a hundredweight of biscuit. He brought me also a box of sugar, a box of flour, a bag full of lemons, and two bottles of lime juice, and an abundance of other things. But, besides these, and what was a thousand times more useful to me, he brought me six clean, new shirts, six very good neckcloths, two pairs of gloves, one pair of shoes, a hat, one pair of stockings, and a very good suit of clothes of his own, which had been worn very little. I can assure you that the clothes felt very awkward and uneasy upon me at first.

After all these things were brought into my little apartment, we began to consult what was to be done with the prisoners we had, and whether we might venture to take them away with us or not, especially two of them, whom we knew to be incorrigible and refractory to the last degree. The captain said that he knew they were such rogues that there was no trusting them. If he did carry them away, it must be in irons, as malefactors, to be delivered over to justice, at the first English colony he could come to. Upon this, I told him that I would undertake to bring the two men he spoke of to make it their own request that he should leave them upon the island, of which the captain said he should be very glad.

I accordingly sent for them, and entered seriously into discourse with them upon their circumstances. One of them answered in the name of the rest, that they had nothing to say but this, that when they were taken, the captain promised them their lives, and they humbly implored my mercy. But I told them that I knew not what mercy to show them, for, as for myself, I had resolved to quit the island with all my

men, and had taken passage with the captain to go to
England. The captain would not carry them to England, except as prisoners in irons, to be tried for mutiny and running away with the ship. The consequence of this, they must needs know, would be the
gallows. I could not tell which was best for them,
unless they had a mind to take their fate in the island.
If they desired that, as I had liberty to leave the island,
I had some inclination to give them their lives, if they
could shift on shore. They seemed very thankful for
it, and said that they would rather venture to stay
there than to be carried to England to be hanged.

I then told them that I would let them into the
story of my living there, and put them into the way
of making it easy for them. Accordingly I gave them
the whole history of the place, and of my coming to
it. I showed them my fortifications, the way I made
my bread, planted my corn, cured my grapes, and in
a word, all that was necessary to make it easy for
them. I told them the story of the Spaniards that
were to be expected, for whom I left a letter, and
made them promise to treat them in common with
themselves.

I left them five muskets, three fowling pieces, and
three swords. I had about a barrel and a half of powder, which I left them. I gave them a description of
the way I managed the goats, and directions to milk
and fatten them, to make both butter and cheese. In
a word, I gave them every part of my own story. I
told them that I would prevail with the captain to

leave them two barrels of gunpowder more, and some garden seeds, which I told them I would have been very glad of. Also I gave them the bag of peas which the captain had brought me, and bade them to be sure to sow and increase them.

Having done this, I left them the next day, and went on board the ship. The next morning two of the five men came swimming to the ship's side, and making a most lamentable complaint of the other three, begged to be taken into the ship, for God's sake, for they should be murdered.

The captain pretended to have no power without me, but, after some difficulty, and after their solemn promises of amendment, they were taken on board, and were soundly whipped, after which they proved very honest and quiet fellows.

Some time after this, I went with the boat on shore, the tide being up, with the things promised to the men, with which the captain, at my intercession, sent their chests and clothes, which they were very thankful for. I also encouraged them, by telling them that if it lay in my way to send any vessel to take them in, I would not forget them.

When I quitted this island, I carried on board, for relics, the great goat's-skin cap I had made, my umbrella, and one of my parrots. Also I did not forget to take the money I had laid by me so long useless.

And thus I left the island the 19th of December, by the ship's account, in the year 1686, after I had been upon it twenty-eight years, two months, and nineteen days. I was delivered from the second captivity the same day of the month that I had made my escape from among the Moors at Sallee.

In this vessel, after a long voyage, I arrived in England, the 11th of June, in the year 1687, having been thirty-five years absent.

When I came to England I was as perfect a stranger as if I had never been known there. My benefactor and faithful steward, with whom I had left my money in trust, was still alive, but had had great misfortunes in the world. She had become a widow the second time, and was in very low circumstances. I made her easy as to what she owed me, assuring her that I would give her no trouble. On the contrary, in gratitude to her former care and faithfulness to me, I relieved her as much as my little stock would afford, which at that time would indeed allow me to do but little for her. I assured her that I would never forget her former kindness to me, nor did I forget her when I had sufficient to help her at a later time.

I went down afterward into Yorkshire, but my father was dead, and my mother, and all the family extinct, except two sisters, and two of the children of one of my brothers, and, as I had been long ago given over for dead, there had been no provision made for me, so that, in a word, I found nothing to relieve or assist me, and the little money I had would not do much for me when it came to settling in the world.

I met with one piece of gratitude, indeed, which I did not expect. The master of the ship, whom I had

so happily delivered, gave a very handsome account
to the owners of the manner in which I had saved the
lives of the men and the ship. Accordingly, they
invited me to meet them and some other merchants
concerned, and all together they made me a very
handsome compliment upon the subject, and a present
of almost two hundred pounds sterling.

But, after I had reflected upon the circumstances
of my life, and how little way this would go toward
settling me in the world, I resolved to go to Lisbon,
and see if I could get any information of the state of
my plantation in the Brazils, and of what had become
of my partner, who, I supposed, had for some years
now given me up for dead.

With this view, I took shipping for Lisbon, where
I arrived the following April. My man Friday accompanied me very honestly in all these ramblings,
and proved a most faithful servant upon all occasions.
When I came to Lisbon, I found by inquiry, and to
my particular satisfaction, my old friend, the captain
of the ship, who first took me up at sea, off the shore
of Africa. He had grown old and had left the sea.
His son now captained the ship, and still carried on
the Brazil trade. The old man did not know me, and
I scarcely knew him, but he soon recollected me
when I told him who I was.

After some passionate expressions of our old acquaintance, I inquired after my plantation and my
partner. The old man told me that he had not been

in the Brazils for about nine years, but that he could
assure me that, when he came away, my partner was
living, but the trustees, whom I had appointed with
him to watch over my part, were both dead. However, he believed that I should have a very good account of the improvement of the plantation. In the
general belief of my being cast away and drowned,
my trustees had given in the account of the produce
of my plantation to the procurator fiscal, who had
appropriated it, in case I never came to claim it, one-
third to the king, and two-thirds to the monastery of
St. Augustine, to be expended for the benefit of the
poor. If I appeared, or anyone for me, to claim the
inheritance, it would be restored, except the improvement, or annual production, which, as he said, had
been distributed to charitable uses, and he thought
could not be restored.

I was a little concerned and uneasy at this account,
and inquired of the old captain how it came to pass
that the trustees should thus dispose of my effects,
when they knew that I had made my will, and made
him, the Portuguese captain, my universal heir. He
told me that that was true, but as there was no proof
of my being dead, he could not act as executor, until
some certain account should come of my death. Besides, he was not willing to intermeddle with a thing
so remote. It was true that he had registered my will
and put in his claim, and, could he have given any
account of my being dead or alive, he would have

acted by procuration, and taken possession of my ingenio (the sugarhouse), and given his son, who was now in the Brazils, orders to do it.

The old man then asked me if he should tell me how to make my claim to the plantation. I told him that I thought to go over to it myself. He said that I might do so if I pleased, but that if I did not, there were ways enough to secure my right, and immediately to appropriate the profits to myself. As there were ships in the river of Lisbon just ready to go to the Brazils, he made me enter my name in a public register, with his affidavit, affirming, upon oath, that I was alive, and that I was the same person who took up the land for planting the said plantation at first. This being regularly attested by a notary, and a procuration affixed, he directed me to send it, with a letter of his writing, to a merchant of his acquaintance at the place. He then proposed my staying with him till an account came of the return.

Never was anything more honorable than the proceedings upon this procuration. In less than seven months I received a large packet from the survivors of my trustees, the merchants for whose account I went to sea, and, as the Brazil ships all come in fleets, the same ships which brought my letters brought my goods, and the effects were safe in the Tagus before the letters came to my hands. By these it appeared that I was now master, all of a sudden, of more than five thousand pounds sterling in money, and had an

estate, as I might call it, in the Brazils, which brought
in more than a thousand pounds a year, as safe as any
landed estate in England. In a word, I was in a condition which I could scarcely understand, and I did
not know how to compose myself for its enjoyment.

The first thing I did was to recompense my original
benefactor, my good old captain, who had been charitable to me in my distress, kind to me in the beginning, and honest to me at the end. I showed him all
that was sent me. I told him that, next to the Providence of heaven, which disposes all things, it was
owing to him, and that it now lay on me to reward
him. So I sent for a notary, and caused him to draw
a procuration, empowering the captain to be my re-
ceiver of the annual profits of my plantation, and
appointing my partner to account to him, and make
the returns by the usual fleets to him, in my name.
I added a caluse at the end, making a grant of one
hundred moidores* a year to him during his life, and
fifty moidores a year to his son after him, for his life.
Thus I requited my old man.

After a time I returned to England and I took my
two nephews, the children of one of my brothers, into
my care. The elder having something of his own, I
brought up as a gentleman, and gave him a settlement
of some addition to his estate after my decease. The
other I put out to the captain of a ship, and, after five
years, finding him a sensible, bold, enterprising young

---

* A moidore is a former Portuguese gold coin.

fellow, I put him into a good ship, and sent him to sea. And this young fellow afterward drew me in, old as I was, to farther adventures myself.

In the meantime I in part settled myself here. For, first of all, I married, and had three children, two sons and one daughter.

Friday lived with me and we never forgot our days upon the island. For many years the sea called to me day and night and often I longed for new adventures.

Thus I have given the first part of a life of fortune and adventure—a life of Providence's checkerwork and of a variety which the world will seldom be able to show the like of. It began foolishly, but it closed much more happily than any part of it ever gave me leave so much as to hope for.